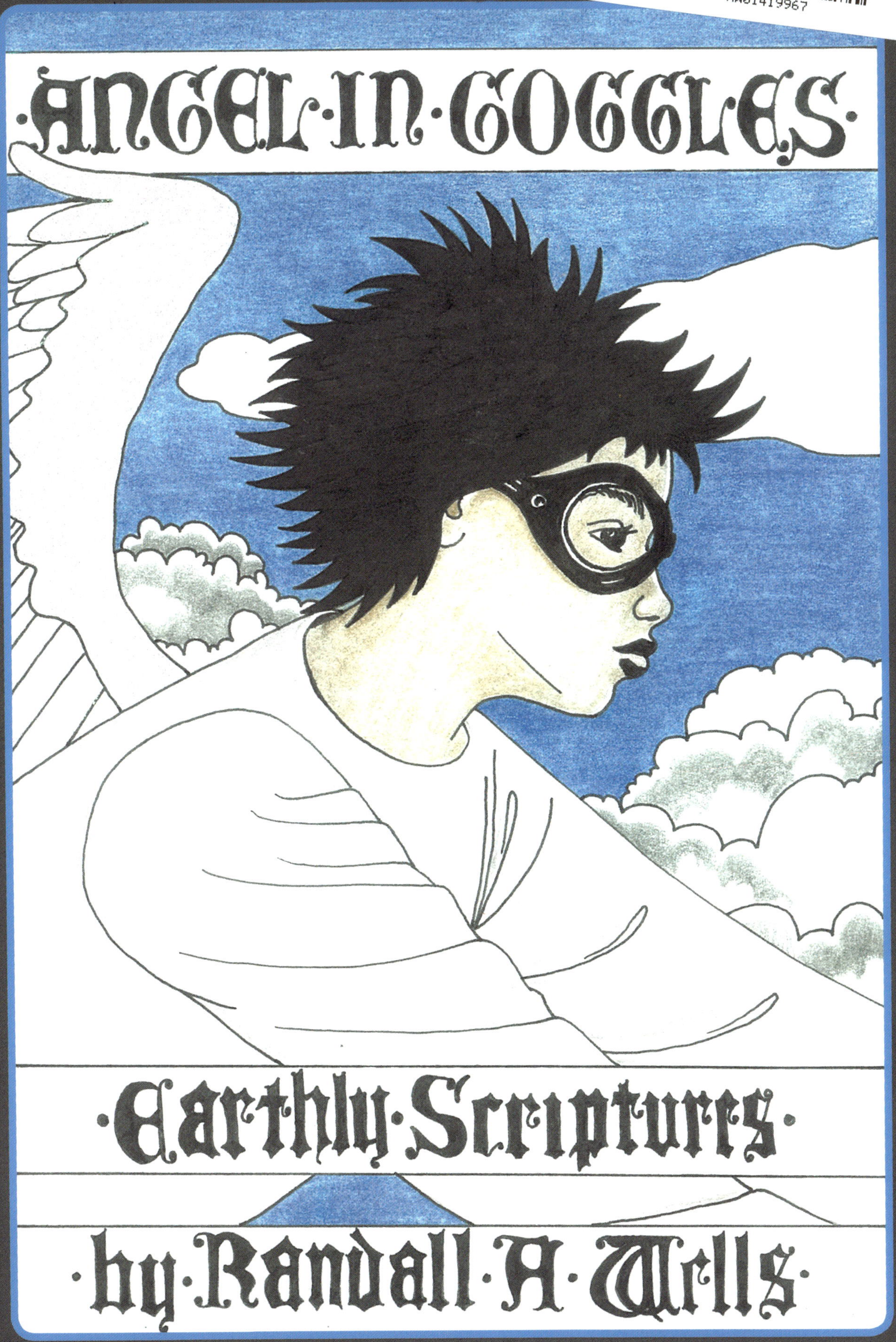
·Angel·In·Goggles·
·Earthly·Scriptures·
·by·Randall·A·Wells·

Also by the author:
Along the Waccamaw: A Yankee Discovers a Home by the River.
Chapel Hill, NC: Algonquin, 1990.
Stretch: Explore, Explain, Persuade.
Upper Saddle River, NJ: Prentice Hall, 1998.
Swamp, Strand, & Steamboat:
Voices of Horry County, South Carolina, 1732-1954.
Conway, SC: Horry County Historical Society, 2004.
Old Times in Horry County: A Narrative History.
Charleston, SC: The History Press, 2007.
Floydiana.
An e-book, www.randallawells.com
Wells also directed the Horry County Oral History Project. He has studied or taught at nine colleges or universities.
Copyright Randall A. Wells 2012, 2015.

Copyright © 2017 by Randall A. Wells. 767986

ISBN:	Softcover	978-1-5434-5225-9
	EBook	978-1-5434-5226-6

All rights reserved. No part of this book may be reproduced or transmitted in any form or by any means, electronic or mechanical, including photocopying, recording, or by any information storage and retrieval system, without permission in writing from the copyright owner.

Print information available on the last page

Rev. date: 10/18/17

To order additional copies of this book, contact:
Xlibris
1-888-795-4274
www.Xlibris.com
Orders@Xlibris.com

November 2017

With thanks to Fred First —
The Christian tech perennial
behind the atheist Angel —

Your pal —
Randall A. Wells

To Sidney Wells Vasaune

*Nothing is holy,
much is precious.*

The Angel Unfaith

Acknowledgements
Version of 2011

I thank Marjory Wells for waiting out another prolonged creative frenzy inseparable from drudgery, for giving me advice as tactful as it was valuable, and for reminding me not to hunch over the computer.

Thank you, Paul O. Zelinsky, for what approaches a collaboration on the *Rapunzel* chapter.

Even a seer can be astigmatic. So for their help I thank friends and relatives in a dozen states from Hawaii to Florida:

Jane Cundiff, Marie Henry, Amanda Hollinger, Joanne C. Irvin, Dennis Ross, Andrea Vasaune, and Carol Widmer, who wrote comments throughout the ever-changing manuscript. For making incisive recommendations about part of the book I thank Richard O. Collin and Marilyn Rutter (proofreader, too). And for sharing their responses to one or more of these chapters: Nora Hollinger, Alan Grindal, and Lynn Carden. Also Jennifer Albright, Reggie Daves, Mike Duff, Jeff Eggart, Ann First, Fred First, Elizabeth Grob, Jim Henderson, Linda Henderson, Tom Hollinger, Merry Macke, Joanie Oakes, Joan Piroch, Becky B. Pomponio, Anna Siegler, Dudley C. Wells, Katie Wells, Ted Walkup, Emily Williamson, and Allison Faix (Reference Librarian).

I also thank the late Virginia Stone of the *Glen Ellyn News* (Illinois) for agreeing to print the bi-weekly travelogues that would become the main source for several chapters fifty years later. And I honor the late Prof. Carolyn L. Blair for listening to the first version of "Erzerum Coming" as I read it from a yellow legal pad in 1962. My appreciation also goes to the *Field & Herald* (Conway, South Carolina) for printing the original stray-mutt account in 1978.

For valuable source-material: Tom Hollinger, Fred First, Renée Smith, Anna Siegler, and Jenny Olsen. In 1961-62 Tom took most of the *National Geographic*-like photographs on 35 mm Kodak film; about halfway between then and now he had the wit to rescue these slides from the dusty clutches of time by digitalizing them on a high-quality scanner.

To my fellow alphabeteer, Fred, I express gratitude for his patience and computer expertise. Out on Goose Creek Run, farthest outpost of InDesign, I spent many a congenial hour transferring red-scrawled changes from printouts to one final electronic version after another.

Version of 2015

I thank the late Henry J. Firley for assigning a journal during my last semester at Glenbard West High School, 1960. Continued for more than fifty years, by pen and eventually pixel, it became a major source for this book.

I am grateful to several people who guided *Angel* through various manifestations. Jill Darlington-Smith was able to extract the original Microsoft Word version from the InDesign document of 2011 so that I could modify it. Fred First thought to translate that document into plain text format because of its anomalies of spacing and typography. Once revised, the Word manuscript was recast in ePub format by Jamie Reygle.

For technical help I once again thank Fred—Buhminham's finest.

And again I thank Marjory for being so patient, or at least resigned. "All I see is your back," she once complained. The author's affectionate reply: "Always delighted to see you in my book."

Foreword

These scriptures are earthbound. Gravel, gravity, grandson. Their only concession to the otherworldly is a winged figure who sports practical eye-gear. Even your author is less prophet than monk, bespectacled and time-tonsured. And he is more entertainer than seer.

What follows is an earthly testimonial by an author (b. 1942) who recognizes nothing transcendent or immanent. Gaia, he believes, is a material girl. She's all we have and all we get. Mystery, yes; magic, no. Wonder, yes; worship, no. (Adore has a knob.) Spirited, yes, not spiritual—a word equally pleasant and vague.

Angel has a secular-humanist edge but not a polemical intention. It has no interest in changing anyone's mind. The author, however, does have a rather astringent intellectual bent (or spiritual scoliosis), so, as he likes to quip, he can apply the standards of reason to the behavior of others.

These pages draw largely upon his three-score-and ten, as well as upon his begetters. From his father, Dudley (b. 1914), he inherited a measure of joie de vivre laced with impish deadpan. Betty, his mother (b. 1918), was much appreciated for her droll repartee, but she would often note the untimely, the untoward, the unfair: "It's a crime!" The author, too, refuses to keep on the sunny side of life despite a song that's inadequately woeful. He does treasure the bright side, in part because it can be so rare and fragile.

He also has a high regard for magnanimity, Aristotle's "crowning virtue" of being great of mind and heart. "They're *good* people," my mother once declared, taking a thoughtful puff from her cigarette; "But they're not *big* people."

As with the Christian bible, the canon of *Angel* admits an assortment of types and lengths. But this variety promises recurrent themes, objects, phenomena, and characters.

One early chapter takes an inventory of the Window—an artifact that illustrates the world's extreme degree of sensory, concrete variegation. "The moon it's not."

A half-dozen intermittent chapters compose a knapsack travelogue. Besides reporting details about places, people, and adventures, it traces an over-up-down-and-around course that attests to the world's shape as a globe.

This sequence complements another, a record of life on Randall and Marjory's "Estate." These chapters tend to cherish the place's topography, terrain, flora, fauna, weather, seasons, and heavens. Both series offer contrary ways of experiencing the earth: locomotion vs. location, wander vs. Walden.

Angel also gives a full weather report with its story about the young author who gets caught between fresh snow and ethical gray. Other chapters explore the conflict between public and private property. One of them analyzes the book *Rapunzel*, by Paul O. Zelinsky. This chapter also celebrates Art as valuable to earthlings.

Angel has a keen interest in the relationship between humans and other species. An entire chapter investigates the dog—often a sacred cow with a collar.

How do humans and other vertebrates monitor their balance and bodily positions, especially against gravity? A chapter admires proprioception, usually neglected as not one of the Five Senses.

And what about the relationship of this earthly speck to the supernal? *Angel* concludes with a nigh-hallucinatory Revelation.

Table of Contents

Foreword 5

1. Geodyssey I: First Gear 8

2. Abstangibles: The Window 10

3. Geodyssey II: Over the Top Underground 23

4. The Estate I: Marmon, Margin 27

5. Snowfallen World 37

6. Geodyssey III: "Erzerum Coming!" 39

7. Like A Member of the Family 45

8. The Estate II: Snouts & Louts 59

9. Private vs. Public: Don't Pass, You Pass 63

10. Geodyssey IV: The Sewer of Despond 67

11. Proprioception: "We Have Hefted the Plates" 72

12: The Estate III: "Stoney Reality" 81

13. Geodyssey V: Longitude 88 E 88

14. The Estate IV: "World Ball" 95

15. Rapunzel: The Child for the Plant 105

16. The Estate V: Free of Earth, Bound to It 110

17. Geodyssey VI: "Curve Ahead!" 114

18. Unfaith Drops In 122

1. Geodyssey I: First Gear

From on high I watch the top of my father's tan Chevrolet Corvair as it weaves in and out of the traffic in search of us.

On October 2, 1961, Tom and I posed for a photograph by the grandfather's clock, then hauled our luggage into the car. Dad drove us from our suburb around the outskirts of Chicago to the Indiana Toll Road. At the oasis-restaurant he ducked in for a cup of coffee, perhaps reluctant to abandon us (only a year after he and my mother had driven me to college). In the lobby we each stuck out a thumb toward people going outside, who glanced at our boots and the pile surrounding us: bedrolls, attaché cases holding dress clothes, and knapsacks with an American flag sewn on the backs.

"Don't bother to ask truckers," I declared, "they're not supposed to pick up riders anyway." Ignoring my wisdom, Tom exhorted a pair who had stopped to listen while I rushed to head off a third, apparently their ranking member. The duo said they were afraid of the Ohio police, kept asking the other man if they should take us to New York City.

We stood around. Tom and I offered to chip in on tolls, and I added that I was reputable and my mother loved me. They conferred quietly, said "No." "OK, thanks," we replied politely and slowly turned around toward the crowd of salesmen leaving the restaurant. But as I glanced back toward the far door, I heard one of the drivers say resignedly, "Come on." I poked Tom, almost hollered, each of us now grabbing his stuff, I dropping my winter jacket, my buddy laughing, and out we stumbled. "One o' you come with me, you c'n go with either o' them." Outside I looked up at an immense moving van.

First gear enabled the tractor-trailer to budge across that opening inch of Indiana far below. As the machine dragged eastward, the driver continued through second, third, and on up to about fifteenth. He never uttered a word to the stowaway amid the roar, groan, and crank. Now the other truck labored around us and I saw Tom waving. I wanted to swing my arms and yell, "We did it! We're off!" but feared to call attention to myself lest the driver change his mind. Now through the right pane of the divided windshield my eyes followed the Corvair. Occasionally glancing sidelong at my taciturn chauffeur, I could have said, "That's my father—would you just give your horn a tap?" But after a mile or so the car exited, crossed leftward over a bridge directly above us, and headed toward the city and work.

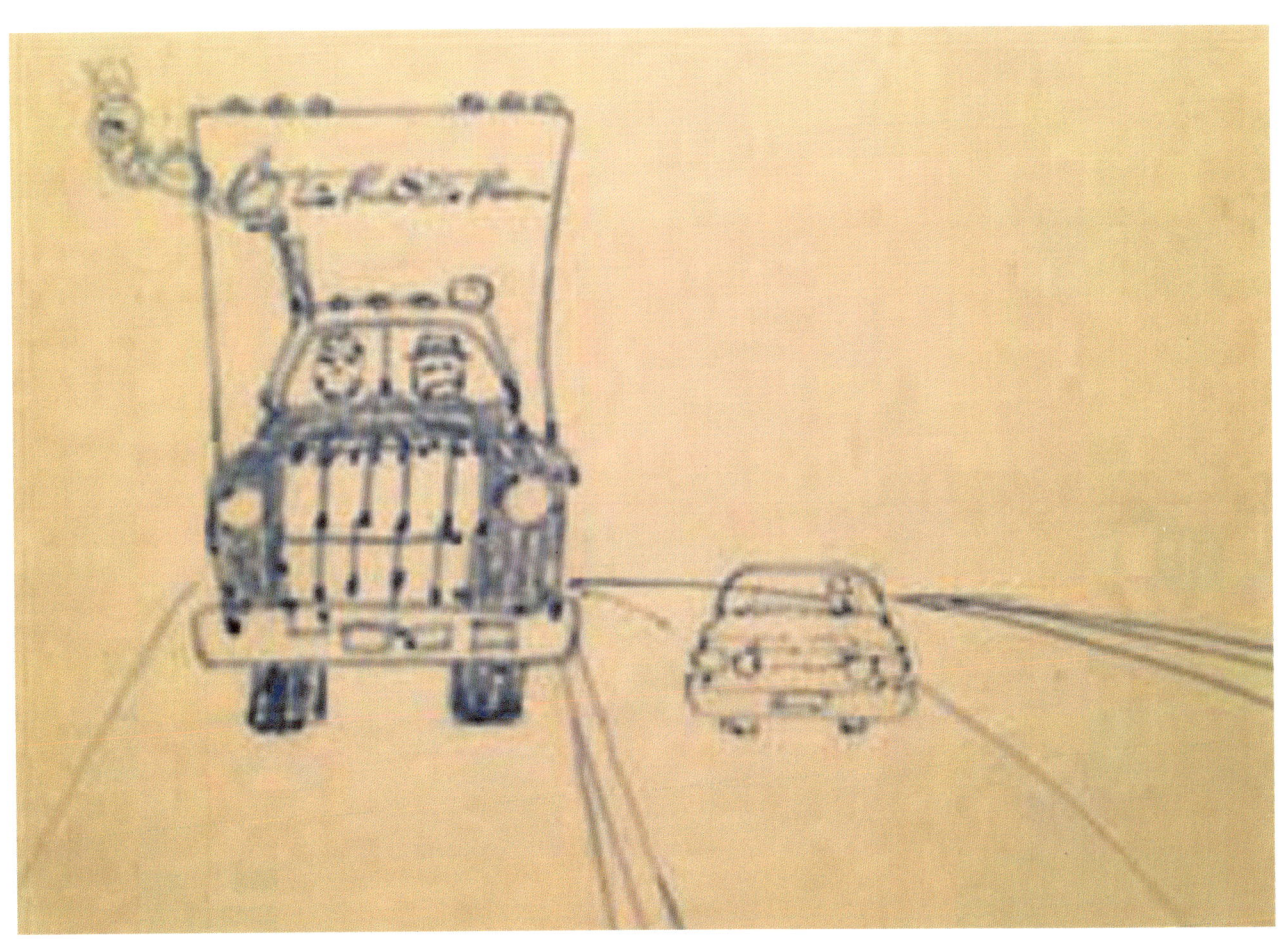

All sketches by the author, 1962.

2. Abstangibles: The Window

For He brought things into being in order that His goodness might be communicated to creatures, and be represented by them; and because His goodness could not be adequately represented by one creature alone, He produced many and diverse creatures, that what was wanting in one in the representation of the divine goodness might be supplied by another. For goodness, which in God is simple and uniform, in creatures is manifold and divided; and hence the whole universe together participates the divine goodness more perfectly, and represents it better than any single creature whatever.

Thomas Aquinas, *Summa Theologica*. London: Burns, Oates & Washburne, 1920, Q. 47, Art. 1, p. 257.
California Digital Library.

Thomas builds on the ancient idea of plenitude—i.e., endless categories and subcategories of earthly beings. Of course this static view is itself "simple and uniform": it doesn't reckon with the plastic and provisional nature of species, entities that in a sense create their variations and descendants. From the howling wolf came the wild New Zealand singing dog.

So Thomas' theory doesn't account for extinct flora or fauna that are predecessors or closely related to living species such as *pelecypods* and *Homo sapiens* (related to *Homo habilis* and *Homo neanderthaliensis*). Little did he dream that human ancestors figuratively swim around in the body—as explained by *Your Inner Fish*.**(1)** In another limitation, Thomas's deity is sentimental. He fashions his own reindeer, so to speak—but not the wolves that prey on them. Or the microbes that cut short many a chance to participate in divine goodness. And did he who made the hemlock make the wooly adelgid?

Still, plenitude of a dynamic kind does characterize the earth. Of course this system includes people. Examples spring to mind: the Prime Ministers of the Fifth Republic, France, about 260 of them **(2)**, and the diverse population of Chile: "Spanish, Irish, English, German and Scottish immigrants, as well as Amerindians and mestizos make up the majority.... Among their neighbors are the indigenous Mapuche, a tribe that survived colonization with its traditions intact. The complex history of Chile's settlement has made it possible to find cultural anomalies throughout the country, such as German immigrants who spoke Spanish, and a revered national hero named O'Higgins." **(3)**

Such variety also extends to all phenomena, whether natural, man-made, or a combination. Examples: shades of green, species of *Phyteuma* (rampion); postage stamps, knots, human genes that show signs of recent evolution (at least several hundred).**(4)** Buttons, bullets, baubles hanging from rearview mirrors, the author's retired neckties, apples (7500 known cultivars—*Wikipedia*), recipes for chicken & dumplings (Deep South, Appalachian, Chinese…), rhetorical schemes as *chiasmus* and rhetorical tropes such as *anapodoton*. Not to overlook languages themselves (extinct as well as living and changing), fiddle tunes, and guitars.

A catalogue for *Musician's Friend*, November 2015, pictured about 366 acoustic and electric models. One example (a further degree of specificity) is the AXS Dread Quilt Ash. It has a quilt ash top/body, set mahogany C-neck, rosewood fingerboard, 3-ply body binding, abalone rosette, 25 ½ scale, with these finishes available—gloss natural, trans-blue, tobacco sunburst or trans black.

Other crowded categories: *asenas* in yoga, sexual positions, football plays, and New Age crystals. *The Crystal Bible* defines two hundred of these stones. Ranging from the precious diamond to the ubiquitous quartz, and from the raw to the cut-and-polished, each has a unique color, shape, size, degree of rarity, and source; and each affects the mind, emotions, spirit, and healing process.**(5)**

Other examples of multiplicity: motels called "El Rancho," instruments of torture, fly-fishing lures….

And train-rail sections. If you torch through a rail vertically and inspect an end, it resembles a goblet. The top is the *head,* which has contact with the wheels, including their flanges, which hug the inside of each rail. The rising part is the *web.* And the base, anchored to the ground, is the *foot.* Of these sections there are hundreds of types—past and present, shapes and weights.**(6)**

What about the locomotive itself that feels its way along the rails, fasteners, ties, ballast, and subgrade? This machine also rides a ladder of subdivisions: *Transportation—by Land—by Rail—Propulsion.* How far down can the hierarchy of general-to-specific reach?

After taking their grandson on a railroad excursion, Randall and Marjory brought home a souvenir book. One of its photographs shows a locomotive. Which type? Diesel. But which sub-type? According to the caption, "General Purpose 4000." One of its particulars distinguishes it from other GP 4000s: its owner, the L&N Railroad, later merged-and-absorbed into oblivion.

Defining the machine has a complication that involves the calendar. Over the years, this GP changes from factory to scrap-tory, so it manifests countless versions of itself. Only when apprehended at any given moment does it seem to have a solid fixedness. According to a photo, this engine existed as one of its ephemeral aspects on March 10, 1979, in the yard of the Southern Railway, Murphy, North Carolina. Each version of the engine, furthermore, is subjective, personal, so as many engines exist as observers and observations. Another challenge to defining invokes physics: this heavy mass is a mystery of atoms, quarks & quiddities.

Leaving aside this subatomic dimension, I'll call the L & N's GP 4000 both concrete and abstract. A compendium of sensory signals, this fume-throbbing, horn-blaring, heat-spreading, rail-stressing, ton-tugging equivalent of four-and-a-half miles of horses bears two headlights and two yellow capital letters in red squares.[7] Yet it's also a conception.

What should they be called, these entities, organic or inorganic, which are apprehensible by the senses and seem fixed, yet constantly change? Perhaps Tangestracts? How about Abstangibles?

In yet another degree of complication, sensory ideas can also be understood figuratively. "This train is bound for glory." "Chew the rampion of thought." "The Bread of Life."

This chapter will explore an example of such a trinity, the Window.

Window as clock and vice versa, Musée d'Orsay, Paris.

Its physical exemplars are slammable, breakable, and infinitely subdivide-able. Like St. Thomas's diversity of fauna, this artifact adds sensory richness to life—by furnishing both view and light, by cooling the forehead, by registering a tap of the finger, by resisting the shove of the sash, even by emanating an esthetic stain. Like most things earthly, a window can serve for good or ill. ("Sometimes hard to distinguish," said the ax to the neck.) No windows in heaven, where light is everywhere 24/7.

A slightly mystical paradox, this artifact: both aperture and barrier. You can open it and still look through the open window. Closed, it can open onto something. Even a vacancy can be so termed: when two-year-old Sidney was playing with bristle-blocks, he looked through a space and declared, "A window." It exists despite unsettled pronunciation: *windoh* (influenced by spelling), *winduh* (folksy), or *winder* (with a view of the holler).

And although this object usually registers upon the eyes, ears, skin, muscles and joints, it can have a theoretical and metaphorical dimension. The Broken Windows hypothesis links the quality of urban maintenance to its degree of vandalism, disorder, and more serious crime. The Johari Window—envisioned by Joseph Luft and Harrington Ingham—is a four-paned theory of personal awareness (open, hidden, blind, and unknown). In my basement scriptorium the only panes are Windows.

Glass itself is an everyday miracle. Technically a liquid, it "creeps" (i.e., slowly thickens toward the bottom at the pull of gravity). It usually begins as undifferentiated silicates, the largest class of minerals, which is melted, then cooled before it crystallizes and becomes a breakable liquid. Does this process not deserve its own holy rite? One ceremony did actually exist, according to a stone tablet that your prophet discovered somewhere and must have put into safekeeping somewhere else. Broken into nineteen fragments and inscribed in Akkadian hieratic, it was dated about 2900 B.C. With due modesty he offers a partial reconstruction:

Proceed under the Thrower-Catcher [i.e., the Big Dipper, so named after a variant of the lacrosse stick with its mesh open to the North Star]. Suspend the [illegible] upon shoulders lined with fur of the [animal of unknown species, single occurrence of word in the corpus, perhaps the orange-coated *Hypax legomenon*]. Slave-tended blaze, black shadow-flickers, sharp-cut-bead gleam. Mix triune [i.e., what glassmakers call "the batch," perhaps composed of silica sand, soda ash, and limestone] weighed by priestly hands. [A lacuna at broken edge of tablet, probably the description of, or prescription for, a refractory pot] upon cedar, mountain-dragged, criss-cross-stacked, sun-storing, sun-dried. Chant the Holy Melt [literally the "un-drying," word usu. found in context of prayer for annual flood]. Hail, fair-visaged, what hast a-cookin'? Sanctify this earthly baseness [literally "unbaked brick," akin to Punjabi *cutcha*, figuratively "of inferior quality" (contrast *pukka*, "baked," a superior building material, "superior"]. Enter, O Tangible-Invisible!

Holy or not, glass can be smooth, rippled, beveled, dimpled or barred; transparent, translucent, colored, and even tinted for shade, color, or privacy. A poor window stimulated the rich imagination of a pig as he looked out his study:

"The windowpanes were frosted up so that he could only see out of the upper quarter of them, and they were made of old-fashioned glass that was so crinkly and full of bubbles that what he did see through them was so twisted and warped that it was hard to tell what it really was. Of course Freddy rather liked this. He said it made the things he saw twice as interesting as they really were. If, for instance, his friend Charles, the rooster, went by, his neck might be drawn out long, so that he looked like an ostrich, or his head might be completely disconnected from his body and float along above him. Whereas seen through a clear pane of glass he was just Charles, and nothing to think about much."(8)

Clean or dirty, a window can be heated, painted, painted shut, frosted, or fake. A stuck-on grille can make a lone sheet of glass seem to comprise smaller ones. Although some windows are sealed, others can be raised, lowered, slid, or swung—horizontally or vertically, by a cranking hand, a hooking pole, or a button-pushing finger. Arms pulling down a sash may feel the extra resistance (by hidden counterweights that keep the window from slamming down when up). In a treasured memory, our daughter Katie boarded the train from Grenoble to Lyon and disappeared inside—where her almost-nine-year-old hands struggled to raise a window and wave away my forlornness.

This artifact can let in fresh or keep out cold air, or even keep in all air (of a space capsule). A window can itself be windowed by an insulating pane or a storm glass. The windshield of a modern vehicle is a sandwich of plastic spread between two sheets of glass. This substance readily admits waves that travel at 186,000 miles a second but muffles those at 761 miles per hour. It invites a passer-by to shop (*lécher les vitrines*, "to lick the windows"), and it displays anything from Belgian waffles to Turkish prostitutes. A window can reflect the out-looker from inside, especially when the outside is dark and the inside light; and also the in-looker, when the glass creates a two-dimensional Outside. When intentionally one-wayed, glass lets the in-looker be undetected by suspects or subjects.

Any window lets the out-looker be unseen when in a dark room, behind a curtain, or behind reflected sunlight. In *La Jalousie*, a novel by Robbe-Grillet (1957), the narrator spends a lot of time peering through a louvered window to observe (or imagine) the conduct of his wife and neighbor. Indeed, framed glass is a window of opportunity for a peeper. It can also serve as a door—for a keyless owner, a lover, or an intruder. It can be a means of protection and a cause of injury by slam or shard. It can offer an escape from death or an escape from life. Fish dart near the transparent window-bottom of a tour boat; birds flap across a skylight.

Some windows are even interior. They can display frozen pizzas in a grocery store, goodies in a patisserie, a diorama in a museum, a newborn in a hospital, a cake in an oven, a wood-fire blazing, a set of china sparkling. In one restaurant, a trio of multiple-pane windows hangs down the middle of a room, at varied distances from floor, ceiling, and one another; they artfully separate the pan-roasted giant Gulf white prawns from the spring vegetable gnocchi. Even along the subway platform, recessed cases advertise products or events. Even furniture can have a window, such as the clock that was a twenty-fifth anniversary present to my mother's grandmother, Sophia. Through its tall, transparent door little Andrea stared at her brass reflection in the disk of the pendulum.

Glass is a canvas for Jack Frost to paint with a gloved hand. A commercial window can provide the backing for a sign, and it can verify an earthquake by undulating. Any window can record a child's handprint or flatten a child's nose to a gastropod. A decal on the front windshield can give access to a military reservation or a parking space; a rear windshield can honor a deceased person; either windshield can receive radio signals with an in-glass antenna. Moving windows? They turn the world to a movie, as when the Indiana Toll Road passed before and beneath the moving van. Time-lapse photography? The porthole overlooking the dock of Boston Harbor at night encircles the dock of Halifax in the morning.

The frame of any window—square, round, fan-shaped—creates proto-art.

For example, in the author's photograph to the left, the glass allows a view of Chicago's Michigan Avenue. But the window's vantage point on the 34th floor also determines the view. It emphasizes height, both downward and upward; and its oblong shape emphasizes the tall facades of the skyscrapers. Its shape and elevation divide the scene roughly into two wedges that are flush with each other—ground-level and up-rising. The window's very

rectangularity emphasizes the diminishing perspective of buildings, their windows, and the avenue by contrasting with the almost complete lack of straight-on right angles. Those constructed with T-squares are foreshortened into lopsihedrons. (Vantage point courtesy Jean-Pierre and Jenny Vasaune.)

In *Desdemona 2010* (below), Gibby Waitzkin framed her photograph with an antique window lattice, white on sepia. This complication divides outside from inside, very private from relatively public, and a weatherworn artifact of many rectangles from a naked young woman. Her long hair cascades through several panes, and she wraps her arms around an already-curved body that presses a bed sheet into radial creases. The grille heightens the woman's youthful sexuality, the mystery of her expression, the electricity of the presumed eye-contact, and the ambiguity as to viewer/viewed. (Pigment print on Sarvisberry-blend handmade paper sealed with beeswax. 45 ½ x 30 in. All rights reserved.)

Romeo's "yonder window" is ubiquitous in literature. One of Faulkner's protagonists conducts an unofficial marriage ceremony in the attic. Afterward "a window that had been dark was lighted and Miss Emily sat in it, the light behind her, and her upright torso motionless as that of an idol."**(9)** An anthropomorphic building can have "vacant eye-like" windows ("The House of Usher," by Edgar Allan Poe, 1839) or it can watch the seasons pass (*The Little House*, written and illustrated by Virginia Lee Burton, 1942).

As for song, that annoying doggie in the window (1952) was finally humped by Elvis's hound (1956). Film? A moviegoer at a drive-in can watch through the windshield as James Stewart looks through the rear window of his apartment and then through his neighbor's. It was curtains for Bonnie and Clyde when they pulled down a shade announcing to pedestrians that the bank was being robbed. And in the ballet *La Sylphide*, the hero glimpses something through the farmhouse window in Act 1 that foretells his ruin. In painting or photography, the image of a window can be doubly framed—by the rest of the scene as well as by the wood or metal around both. The Metropolitan Museum of Art even held a show called "Rooms with a View: The Open Window in the 19th Century" (2011).

One such window ended the career of a pipe organ:

"The old Hook & Hastings was causing many problems, often playing on her own without the organist, and so becoming known as the 'Hasty Hooker.' Finally she had to be dismantled. The pipes were thrown out a third-floor window of the church straight into the dumpster. To help dispose of the console itself, several friends used an axe. One of us would yell something like, 'This is for the time you ciphered during Margaret's wedding!' or 'Remember the time you wouldn't play at all for worship?' and then take a swing."(10)

One night the framed glass of our house in Illinois had dramatic multiple functions. I was staying next door because relatives were visiting, when Greg woke me up after running across the yards and up the stairs. "There's smoke all through the house! We don't know why!" In slippers I galloped into the mild February darkness and peered through a squat basement window—to see grayness split by an angry flicker of orange. After someone called the fire department, my father and I ran across the street to our neighbors' garage and carried back an extension ladder, which we propped against the roof of the front porch. To the faint wail of a siren, people climbed out of the raised sash in nightgowns and pajamas: my brother Cap, my grandmother, my two cousins, and my mother, whose hand bled after smashing the storm-window with a drinking glass. Window as revelation, escape, injury.

It can also be both cause and casualty. While living in Mississippi, I hauled my dumpster-bound garbage along the sidewalk that ran next to the wall of the apartments. An explosion cracked my eardrums and blinded me with a flash. Regaining balance from the other side of the walk, I looked up at barking teeth and frantically scraping nails. Consumed by anger, I lifted the wastebasket and bounced it tentatively against one pane. Then a second time, noting the greater resistance and the rippled reflection from the bonk that I couldn't hear over the din. Third swing harder—shatter! A yipping frenzy of retreat.

This man-made object can help people treat each other as objects. On November 9, 1938, propaganda against Jewish "dogs" provoked a fury of window-smashing. Ernest Lion, the son of a decorated veteran of World War I, stole across Dortmund, Germany, and hid in a freight car:

"Loud, roaring crowds swept through the streets, shouting their slogans…. Once I stuck my head out of the car to see flames shooting up into the sky. It looked like the entire city was on fire…. At dusk everything quieted down, so I left the rail car and walked into the city. They had burned down the synagogue. Jewish store windows were broken. Clothes, hardware, fine porcelain, groceries, whatever was inside those stores was now scattered around on the sidewalks. Some of it was missing due to looting and plundering. The mob had entered our homes and thrown belongings, even entire pieces of furniture, out of the windows. It was almost impossible to walk around town, as the sidewalks were filled with what was once valuable, useful material which had now become trash. Stars of David were painted on the walls of Jewish establishments, and curtains were waving in the cold November wind through empty window frames. What sounded like snow and ice was broken glass that crunched under the feet of passerby."

After Kristallnacht (Night of the Broken Windows), Ernest was rounded up with many others. Locked in old railroad carriages, they were transported to Weimar, and then marched to Buchenwald concentration camp. Surviving, he was released, only to get a ticket to Auschwitz in February 1943. So once again he became what the perpetrators called a *stück*, a "piece." Having beheld windows destroyed, he now endured them denied:

"The carriages were those plump, old-fashioned, brownish-maroon, wooden freight cars with rounded roofs and tall wheels so narrow that it seemed they could not stay on the tracks. Built to carry forty men or eight horses, according to the white painted sign on the doors, they were packed with a hundred men, women, and children. The only heat was provided by the close-packed bodies; no food, water, or windows."**(11)**

In November, 2001, I ventured to look through a rectangular hole cut into a wooden fence. A smoking, twisted and jumbled mass arose four stories high, the remnant of more than a hundred. Burned ventilation tunnels were mangled together with steel beams and fragments of concrete, wood, and glass—perhaps of windows that once topped the world but now headed for the landfill. The yellow boom of a crane picked away at the mound with clunk after clunk, humming, honking, clacking. A woman slid past me as she wept and vanished among the stricken faces.

High above the congregation, the circular window filled with tracery gave me a pleasure that was almost spiritual. I could look above the altar at most of its glass as well as half the collar into which it was set—an off-white cylinder about a yard deep that reflected sunlight already filtered by the leaded design into hues and shapes. This cast pattern was not circular-flat, like the glass, but curved three-dimensionally. It transformed the twelve apostolic petals, outlined in black on the window proper, to splashes of color. Their emblematic objects—key, boat, fish, and goblet, all of them set against finely-wrought decoration—blurred together as kaleidoscopic, elongated droplets. This version seemed dynamic. It called to mind an ocean wave tinged with reds both light and dark, purples and light blues, whites, and yellows and yellow-oranges. As the service continued I even thought of the artifact as set free as if from Urizon, William Blake's god of spiritual arthritis.

The occasion was the hundredth anniversary of the church. Although the bishop's homily was dramatic and engaging, I studied the uncompromisingly black Haitians, two of them refugees from poverty, the others from earthquake. I found time to admire the dark orange hair of a young woman, once a child who had squealed in glee as I pushed her around the hardwood floor in a chair with rollers. I stared at her coiffeur with its combed, thin-grained lushness and occasionally glimpsed an ivory cheek. The man who read the day's scripture had owned the dog whose idea of public address had forced us to move prematurely to a condominium. The son of my former colleagues, once a baby, could look down on everyone as he raised the cross at the head of a procession. One young woman sat with her widowed father, but her mother, so plumply-vivacious, would not see her go to college.

The collection plate weighed down my hand briefly and then eased off into the next person's. During communion I stood out by sitting. What color is the race of agnostics? As the shaft of light slowly moved from one part of the church to another, it seemed to confer a blessing on people. Yet I marveled that my faith had eroded to nothing. Even as a youngster I had felt an aversion to two strains of Christianity: one that would have dried and pressed me between verses, the other that would have squeezed me between institutional bricks. But now in my sixties, my warmth toward a particular denomination and even my belief in a religion had followed the smoke from the candles I had extinguished as an acolyte.

As the sun angled higher, light from the window progressed slowly up the right section of pews toward the altar. I remembered how its rich spectrum had once fallen on a woman in an orchid dress; kneeling at the imminent prospect of meeting God, she seemed nothing less than transfigured.

Now a parishioner was hugging my spouse, an esteemed nurse-midwife who had delivered her child. Her husband, the rose window's donor, had lived to see another day filtered through the triple-canopy of Vietnam. And to wonder "Who is the enemy here?" as the United States Government indulged the incompetent South Vietnamese army.

The couple with whom we'd once shared a tent in the frigid air was talking with our old friend, honored today as the former vicar. An even earlier priest lauded former members of the parish for their efforts in the civil rights struggle. The deacon was once a high school girl who had chatted with me when I picked up Andrea from daycare. A sprinkling of widows, divorced people, former students.... Our neighbor and friend who had dumped the Hook & Hastings now played the organ to splinters.

Later I thought back on the gorgeously-wrought glass. Did it not co-opt nature in the service of religion? It reminded me of the cross erected at Noccalula Falls Park,

Alabama—an addition that seemed to claim the spectacular canyon on behalf of Christ, and at the same time to Jesusize the timeless slide of river against rock.

Did the many-hued window not divert the pagan sunlight to endorse theology? Maybe its circle was no more holy than the Tiffany-style shade above my weekly journal that, to alter Shelley's celebrated line, "Stains the white radiance from a bulb." The devout tend to see proof of the maker in nature, but the colored glass took one step further and harnessed it.

For me, this was the Church of St. Secula. A worthy venue, it answered the human need for meaning; the pleasure of companionship; the rite of growing up; the curse of negligence and conflict; the loss of lives natural or tragic; and the blessing of beauty inherited or created.

Footnotes:

1. Neil Shubin, *Your Inner Fish: A Journey into the 3.5-Billion-Year-History of the Human Body.* New York: Pantheon, 2008.
2. Barbara Ann Kipfer, *The Order of Things: Hierarchies, Structures, and Pecking Orders.* New York: Workman, 2008, pp. 269-74.
3. Nathaniel Lande and Andrew Lande. *The Ten Best of Everything: An Ultimate Guide for Travelers,* 3rd ed. Washington, DC: National Geographic, 2012, p. 275.
4. Sandra Aamodt and Sam Wang. *How the Mind Grows from Conception to College: Welcome to Your Child's Brain.* New York: MJF Books, 2011, p. 36
5. Judy Hall, *The Crystal Bible: A Definitive Guide to Crystals.* Cincinnati: Walking Stick Press, 2003.
6. Hugh Hunt, "On the Line." *New Scientist,* Sept. 22-28, 2012, p. 65.
7. Michael George and Frank Strack. *Passage Through Time: A Milepost Guide for the Great Smoky Mountains Railroad,* 2000, p. 33. Photo by Jim King.
8. Walter R. Brooks, *Freddy the Pied Piper.* Illustrated by Kurt Wiese. New York: Knopf, 1946, pp. 3-4.
9. William Faulkner, "A Rose for Emily," 1930. xroads.virginia.edu/~drbr/wf_rose.html
10. Ann Miles, personal correspondence, 2011.
11. *The Fountain at the Crossroad,* 1999, pp. 23-24, 40, 56. Unpublished manuscript held by the Holocaust Museum in Washington, DC. Randall Wells and Suzanne Thompson were honored to help the late Mr. Lion write his autobiography.

3. Geodyssey II: Over the Top Underground

Attached to the tunnel, intermittent lights smear the thick pane near my face. After they slow and cease, I get off the train, and at about 2:45 a.m. wait alone somewhere. Leaning against a trashcan, I almost fall asleep and knock it over at the same time. I peer down the tracks till they end without a glimmer of oncoming headlights.

It was a long way from the top floor of 251 E. 51st St., Manhattan. That apartment, where Tom and I were staying with the parents of our hometown friend Stan, was a long way from the moving van of the previous night. There, as the sun had set on October 3, it left a turquoise reflection off the United Nations Building. Time for us to make use of the eighteen-year-old minimum age for buying alcohol. So down we rode to street level and splurged on a jumbo bottle of burgundy as well as a small one of liqueur.

A single button took us back up to the apartment, where we watched TV with our hosts and polished off the bottle, whereupon I changed from grape to banana. Called for

Tom, looked around, and found him in bed. So I stole the neighbor's chair off the next terrace, set up a TV table for my beverage, and sat inhaling the city. Then I hopped to a little terrace by our pal's room and the kitchen. Opened a window, failed to stifle a laugh at Tom, Batmanned back. Decided I loved New York City so much I needed to explore it. Snuck out and not long afterward came to a subway entrance, where I stepped down, down, and into the first train.

Dim under darkness. An escape from workaday light—such as the solar rays that had baked my stint as a house-insulator. As for my occasional twelve-hour overnights at the A & P as a locked-in stock-boy, I was again nocturnal—yet liberated, strangely enough, underground! The dug-out station resembled a mine. And doubly so, because from the earth had come the iron for the steel rails and spikes, as well as the unseen piles of coal that provided electricity for mobility. Not to forget the gravel pit that had supplied ballast.

Aimless, doubly intoxicated, I got off the train somewhere near a place called North Park Ave. Thanks to neon, Pluto's reading lamp, I found a tavern and ordered a martini. Inhaling from a cylinder of decadence, I sipped, I chatted with a fat man and his wife. We talked about Dodgers, who never should have left Brooklyn. This couple had come in to see Larry, a sometime-bartender with asthma whom they had met on last plane trip down from Niagara Falls for the Woild Series. I mentioned how much fun Larry was, especially during the Series. Out the door.

Subterranean again. The name Queens pleased me, so another vertical descent shifted to horizontal. Amid the train's roar-and-squealing speed I chatted with a genial graduate of the University of Illinois ('52) who was seeking his fortune as an architect. I assured him that I was reputable. When we bade farewell, I stepped down from already-down, found another tavern, and ordered a Manhattan. Had a conversation with a fellow who, every time he cracked a joke, patted me on the back, then my arm, then my leg. The old guy, moreover, kept asking me why I had trouble with my landlady, while insisting that he didn't want to pry. Long story? What is it? Oh, I don't want to pry, long story? Bartender looked disgusted, time for me to wobble out.

Down, down again from the emptying street. Again I climbed aboard, in the wrong direction, further into Queens. *Through the mountain hurtled Gilgamesh toward the sunrise, toward the garden paradise, after the death of his friend-like-a-younger-brother Enkidu, but for league after league he saw only darkness in front and behind.* Light returned as moving headlights and blinking neon.

I barely made it into a tavern in time to relieve myself. Walked around a massive animal that lay right in the middle of the aisle, said loudly, "Pardon me, dog." Patrons laughed. Ordered a Manhattan, lit a cigarette (alien activity) and moments later felt an unusual sensation. Reacted with an indefinite motion, then sat calmly while the bartender asked, "You all right, sir? Burn yourself?" The customers looked worried. I replied with insouciance, "No." "You're lucky…. Be a good fellow and put that out." On the floor I spied my matchbook in flames. Got up and put it out with a nonchalant stomp that a Renaissance courtier would recognize as *sprezzatura*. Now sharply feeling my thumb, I immersed it in my cool, antibacterial beverage until I finished sipping and left.

Got to the Elevated station, where I waited for fifteen minutes, again taking a leak, this time perilously close to the third rail. Caught a train in the right direction but got off too early. Stood on the platform another fifteen minutes. Talked with a Chinaman about Red China, doubted he knew what it was, and told him to hate it anyway. Standing at a respectful distance, I assured him as to my reputability. On the noisy train car I asked for his address so I could write and let him know I was OK. He told me I was a good boy and gave me his card: Tom Shong, 239 E. 13th St., New York, New York.

I got off at Park Ave., hiked to the surface, messed around, decided I wanted to see 42nd St. and Broadway. Back down the steps, back on a train, back off it. Waited, waited for a transfer at around quarter to three.

As the trashcan wobbles, I decide "Enough." So I climb to the surface and walk back. On the top floor of the building, I giggle the whole story to Tom, and four hours later we awake. Our hostess calls the doorman and asks him to hail us a cab, and soon the dignified gent is grabbing my knapsack and running toward the yellow sedan that Tom (who had the wit to give chase) has stopped around the corner as the doorman now holds the straps like a big purse, his long legs pumping. A pedestrian jams my drooping strap into the cab window. Not long afterward we are riding an intercity bus, where I recline in a fog, head contesting with stomach, luckily unconscious of the earth's slight curvature northward and eastward until we reach Boston. On the MTA, a lady picks up the tired strap from the floor and tucks it into my backpack. At Vinnie's Sandwich Shop, the owner gives us a free meal. Having slept twenty stories above the land, and taken many a step below it, we now reach the limit of the continent and the wooden piers that stick out from it.

Boryhurst
RJ Hunt

Vinnies Sand Shop
285 Main St.
Camb Mass
James Macaluso
Jos Pocelle   c/o Vinnie Sand
                        Shop
Giorgio Trotta

4. The Estate I: Marmon, Margin

Far above the highway I gaze through old-time split windshield at the long hood of the dump truck, a 1987 Marmon. An extinct brand, its residual blue fades even more in the slipstream, its rivets strain to hold the body together, and its passenger seat gradually lowers as the air leaks, a problem remedied every so often by a screwdriver applied to a notch. Our contractor, Ms. King, goes through about a dozen shifts as we head toward the mulch depot.

A few minutes earlier I had grasped a step welded to the side-borne gasoline tank, angled one leg to get a boot onto the first rung, reached for the side-handle, and stumbled off like a drunk. Another attempt brought access to the cab, which then lumbered down our steep gravel lane with an outrageous ***putt-a-putta*** from its engine brake. This was forty-eight years to the month since Tom and I had each experienced the compound mobility of hitchhiking in a moving van.

After a few years of traveling as often as possible from South Carolina, my spouse and I retired to Virginia, the fifth colored-in-state of our marital atlas. We planned to join Greg and his wife, and he helped me outline the house with twine and stakes. To our clear-cut ridge we imported a flatbed-kit of thick pine logs, but as they were forming a structure, my apparently robust brother pedaled up a mountainside to Beulah Land. He left me with sixty years of memories, among them his role as guitar teacher; our cat-and-mouse automobile chase around the Wyoming-Colorado border; our pilgrimages to a down-and-out bar near the railroad tracks in West Virginia; and an all-day hike undertaken to cool our feet in the Atlantic. What could Marge and I do but continue living in endless absence? We hung a photograph of him as he stood contemplating the landscape through the gap of an uninstalled window. But with time, "We are here without him" shaded into "Without him we wouldn't be here."

We fondly named our house The Cabin, even though its square footage made it a "lodge" in industry parlance. On its east side deck served as the roof of a carport and opened to a shallow valley, formed by Dodd Creek, and a glimpse of Epperly Mill Rd. Above the opposite hills poked the rooftops of a village, where on one building binoculars could make out FARMERS' SUPPLY.

But for intervening trees, the lenses could spot a statue whose height was about two-thirds the length of my walking stick. (Its grip was defined by a dozen whittled lines and the initials G.W.) The beautiful image troubled me. Her serenely swirling solidity, her out-peeking set of bare toes that invited yet coldly rejected a kiss…. She was two steps removed from life: up in heaven and turned to marble. Her own tombstone. Had she lived? Was she, is she mourned?

Could I whisper something in her ear to break a trance? Was she reading Hebrew from right to left? But how could she turn a page? How could she fly? "At least put the book down," I thought, "and hike with me!"

The basement of our new place was a walk-in because the foundation-diggers quit trying to penetrate the Appalachian bedrock. I insisted, with mock posh, that our 7.34 acres be called The Estate. We especially prized our land because it merged with the surrounding woods, the valley, the ridges beyond, and the 360-degree, ever-changing spectacle above.

As for water, none flowed into the top of the Blue Ridge Plateau, just from it. I envisioned hauling a kayak down the old logging trail to Dodd Creek, ducking under the bridge across Rt. 221, reaching the Little River, then the New River, then continuing north to the Kanawha in West Virginia, then to the Ohio, then bending south to the Mississippi and eventually tying up near Café du Monde for beignets. Or of hauling the kayak eight miles in another direction to the crest of the Blue Ridge then—why not attach wheels and zip down to the shore for a seafood platter?

Just as our place hovered between earth and heavens, it also blurred the margin between retirement and retrenchment with nature, between wild and domestic, even between nature and family.

On one of his visits, Sidney got to ride in the Marmon, and at its loud return up the communal driveway, he beamed as he stood in his dad's lap. Determined that he would frolic on the new mulch pile, I mowed around it to eliminate the blackberry bushes. At first he was timid, but with a boosting hand he reached the top, then enjoyed running down the sides for a while even though his pants collected wood-shreds.

Marge, Andrea, and I took him down Annie Lane hill in the red wagon, which he himself pulled much of the way up, stopping to load it with a handful of stones. I knelt beside him and pointed out a nest in a tree, then later to a big grasshopper that was succumbing to autumnal lassitude. On the driveway he and I would look at our shadows, maybe wave at them or let them chase each other. "Where's your shadow?" I once asked him with a hint of urgency; he searched in front of him but couldn't locate what was hiding behind.

Up from nothing went the pole barn, the latest artifact on land that had been hunted, farmed, logged, and bulldozed. First the scraping of topsoil, then the dumping of fill dirt, then the be-ribboned stakes, the giant screw at the front of a buckin'-bronco machine, cement in the holes, eighteen or so posts, crossbeams, trusses, hemlock siding, batten, windows, electric double-doors, and wind-contending roof. This static product would give no hint of the process that created it, which was bustling, social, and noisy: groan of diesel equipment, wham of hammers, screech of saw, clunking lumber, words spoken or yelled, all this heard above songs blaring on the radio.

To make way for topsoil and rake, I plucked stones from a half-acre of sloping land between the well and the lane, remnants of the Rocky Mountains of the East. Had Marjory and I not already lived upon these early upheavals? For their white peaks had eroded from bedrock to boulder, large rock to cobblestone, gravel to pebble to sand. They had entered the geological hourglass and emerged as the coastal plain, which encompassed our yard in South Carolina with its beachy patches that often made me think "Snow!"

On the Estate I dislodged these souvenirs by finger, pry-stone, heavy rake, mattock, and sledge hammer, working for minutes or hours a day. Occasionally a rock would surprise my fingers with warmth as if trying to reptile itself. I quit after a piece of cinnamon candy looked like a red stone. Then a heavy rain exposed more debris and I comprehended that this stuff wasn't on top of the ground, it *was* the ground. Still, our version of Newcastle required a fresh supply for the driveway; so a truck from the local quarry dumped a load that the driver, a genial fellow with an accent as thick as his beard, identified cryptically as "57."

Wanting to acquaint Sidney with facts terrestrial, I talked about gravity. Theory led to application: first we lifted the rock that propped open the basement door for sunlight; then he picked up a handful of 57 and watched it fall to the ground. I hoisted the lad himself and let him go, my arms stopping his descent just in time to draw a cackle of glee. We also turned over some flat rocks in the clay, their own headstones.

Black, brown, gray, or tan, they were sometimes doubled like sandwich-bread or thin-layered like mille-feuille, sometimes flecked with gold or silver. (Blue is too much to ask for credence.) We pulled a couple of them apart and then, wanting to introduce the idea that everything earthly changes, I declared that stones eventually become dirt.

Once at daybreak tiny green leaves levitated in the glass doors between dining table and deck. They twined among a bunch of red grapes, a yellow pear, a purple-streaked blue plum, and amber twins of some other kind of fruit. This vision reflected the leaded-glass lampshade, an heirloom from Sidney's great-grandfather Sidney's grandfather Sidney. The mirrored hues faded as rosy clouds began to silhouette trees against ridge. A subsequent dawn revealed several ranks of hills or mountains. First the dark, roughly-treetop-serrated one; then another across the valley that was lightened by mist as well as sunlight; and then a newly-upthrust range beyond and above that slowly turned into gray clouds against an orange streak.

One morning I reeled up the woven-wood-like curtain over the doors and almost rubbed my eyes. Was God making a royal progress above the town? His presence was signaled through the clouds by beacons that inclined slightly, accompanied parallel lines of gray, and traveled gradually northward as stripes. Another time a bird managed to chirp at the sullen, low-clouded doom of dawn. Once the low-angled sun fell on a wild turkey that poked along stiff-legged while dragging its shadow on the gravel like a paperboy's bag.

We appreciated most of the birds on The Estate, but I sometimes had qualms. Unlike Noah's dove, they flew toward the ark. The more they depended on us—weren't they the less wild? The Estate's doves would scatter histrionically only so far from the wire-hanging chuck-wagon. Our friend Jane Cundiff (her fingers ever on Gaia's pulse) reported that there are more and more crows, sparrows, pigeons and other birds that can survive within human habitats. She added: "Many others that require more natural ecosystems are going extinct." This news also gave me a vague sense of constraint. Reducing the wild-bird community would encroach upon something valuable. Something to do with human freedom. I had to admit it, from *us* (Michael Pollan's concept).

Below is our write-up in an avian advisory:

> ## From *A Yard Bird's Survival Guide*
>
> **Site:** Cleared ridge among hardwoods, evergreens, ornamentals
>
> **Dwelling:** log house, tin roof (green)
>
> **Feeder(s):**
>
>   Caged: 2
>
>   Hopper: 0
>
>   Hummingbird 1 (unreliable)
>
> **Feed(s):** Oil sunflower, none Jan.–Feb.
>
> **Bath:** Water quality & reliability minimal
>
> **Cat(s):** 0
>
> **Note:** Female refills tubes, male useless

Out the kitchen window a crow poked around on the gravel next to a gigantic beetle—which I discerned was actually clinging to the screen. One gang of crows, always blowing their noisemakers, would coast wide-winged down to the ellipse formed by the front driveway. Then they would peck under the bird feeder, admirably aggressive nuisances, sinister waddlers.

One morning Sid watched as I jabbed, squeezed, and pulled up dirt with a post-hole digger. I rammed in a wooden post that we stabilized by putting rocks around its base, and afterward screwed a bluebird-house onto it. The box soon held a nest made partly of bright green grass—which itself soon held a clutch of blue eggs. Months later as Marge and I removed the empty beak-creation, we found a single egg, almost weightless, off to the side.

In the carport some animal, maybe a raccoon, broke the floodlights, probably trying to reach the nest of a barn swallow. The nest remained but the custodian was gone and Marge upset. "I watched you every day," she lamented, "taking care of your babies." We replaced the bulbs and who should return but Mama. Once we parked the car and started toward the basement door when Marge halted: "Well, hello!" We looked at a little bird that crouched in the doorway and stared at us. Finally as Marge reached for the door handle, the visitor zoomed out of a cannon.

A black searchlight would sometimes sweep across the foliage, shadow of a winged mouser. A branch would sometimes bend under red, and look! The apex of that tree—it's a scarlet tanager, unconscious of its Portuguese-Amazonian etymology. Once I reeled up the curtain to behold an emerald creature—"such a form as Grecian goldsmiths make." I whispered "Indigo bunting!" Dark-shiny in the faint light, it pecked the grass amid short, pinkish ground cover and yellow dandelions, one of which it trod on and bent over. Then I spotted another such rarity poking around the herb garden. "Poor Marge," I thought, "still denting her pillow."

One day a couple of unfamiliar patrons bellied up to the seed-bar. Trying to identify them in the *Book of North American Birds*(1), I recognized the brown-headed cowbird. It had been invited by open spaces like ours that were surrounded by woodlands. *Molothrus ater* then laid eggs in the nests of other species, hosts that fed the imposters, which gratefully squeezed their young out of food and space. Like many a sociopath, the cowbird disguised opportunism with innocuousness.

I vowed to trap it or shoot it, or at least get a cowbird-pouncing cat. But I feared the blunder of kudzu (Japanese arrowroot). People introduced this "agent of biological control," term supplied by Fred, to combat changes in the natural environment. An occasional meow did issue from foliage somewhere, one with no modulation of volume, duration, or pitch. But this "cat" would not get rescued—unlike our long-ago pet, one of whose nine lives had registered as a sudden weight on the upside-down lid of a garbage can that I held up from a ladder tilted against a pine trunk.

As I surveyed the sky at breakfast, two quick thumps—one into the high triangle of half-inch-thick faux nature, the other onto the deck. At Marge's insistence I finally went outside with a dustpan and brush. Admiring the iridescent green feathers and dainty claws, I reluctantly noted the comic-strip X on its eye. Then I shoved it onto the pan, which I swung toward the treetops for the bird's last flight.

Marge's former boss and colleague, our friend Reggie, visited from South Carolina. He noted seventeen bird species on the property and wrote them on the back of an envelope. One was a chipping sparrow whose high-pitched sound vibrated at the very threshold of hearing. I was pleased to make out its wee nest tucked into the Colorado blue spruce (*Picea pungens glauca*), especially because I had once spent four hours digging through rocks and in snow flurries to make a hole for the tree—only have the landscaper proclaim that it was too close to the circle driveway. (My surly reaction: "*You* move it then!")

The diversity of Appalachian tree species is among the greatest in the world. *Sassafras albidum* can't decide among three leaf-shapes, and its roots, as Fred explained, add a distinctive flavor to a once-popular tea.

He pulled a leaf from another common type, sweet birch (*Betula lenta*) and applied a fingernail to the stem: "Smell this!"

Yet to amplify the original species we hauled root-balls from a nursery that was too conveniently located at the bottom of the hill. At last I finished spreading mulch around all fifty white pine saplings, once mere seedlings that the forester had planted as a windbreak. To create a surface that was receptive to mulch, I had to push and pull the rotary mower around them, so I first had to lop the surrounding blackberry bushes. Their stalks grew so high that a few resembled saplings. This plant crossed from the Plant Domain to the Animal whenever a thorn struck at my leather coat, or pierced my shirt to evoke an "Ow!" and a fly-baiting drop of blood.

I began to differentiate two species of pine: white (*Pinus strobus*) and Virginia (*Pinus virginiana*). The former was symmetrical, branched like a candelabrum, and smooth of trunk. The latter had rough bark, short needles, and no tincture of blue mixed with its green. Idiosyncratic, the Virginia branches thrust out in erratic lengths and patterns, and its trunk could have furnished a boat-mast for the Crooked Man of the nursery rhyme. We were grateful that this species was reclaiming the steep, logged, and stump-burned hill. Another welcome opportunist was the black locust (*Robinia pseudoacacia*). Its dense, thorny trunk was triply territorial as claim-stake, fence post, and barbed wire.

A couple of decades past, loggers had ignored one solitary dead trunk, barkless, gray, a few of its branches sticking out from the very high top. It made a gaunt and even inauspicious first impression on any visitor to The Estate. Yet because of both character and service as a perch, it survived a motion to cut it down (by only one vote, Marge's). Small birds continued to peep from it and large ones to croak silent *Nevermores*. One day a gust transformed the top half into a log. After this lengthy fragment spent time in a bonfire, a remnant emerged as a stub-tailed alligator. (Photo by Jennifer Albright.)

"Is that a holly?" As I was exploring the acreage with our son-in-law Mike, we peered through the gray-brown December tangle to behold a fountain of green-shining leaves. We made our way across the hillside to stand next to the *Ilex opaca* in admiration. No berries—a monochrome male—but robust and cheerful. And near the driveway entrance to the property, what was this conical evergreen volunteer that seemed placed just-so as if by a landscaper? Its berries seemed to identify it as a juniper (*Juniperus communis*)—tiny, blue-white, nasal martinis. It flourished with the aid of hose-water, fertilizer, mulch, and affection.

I also discovered a sole hemlock (*tsuga Canadensis*), a wide-branched species headed for extinction like the American chestnut, once a staple of the region, now a relic as fences, barns, woodwork, and picture-frames. Sure enough, the undersides of the fir's leaves were sprinkled with dots like white smallpox. So I made deep holes around it by pounding a crowbar with a hatchet-head, then injected poisoned water with a turkey-baster. After a month I found no trace of the cuddly-named killers, the wooly adelgids. (In the photo, this tree stands some years later and yards taller, liberated by chain saw from a half-dozen nearby sun-stealers.)

In the spring the dogwoods made their debuts here and there in white gowns. I had trouble distinguishing them from serviceberries (*Amelanchier arborea*), old-time pronunciation "sarvisberries," so named because they blossom around Easter Sunday. In the spring, pines held up votive candles of new growth. While on a visit Tom admired the sea of needles and sprouting leaves: "I tried to count the shades of green but gave up."

I had saved the last two fertilizer stakes out of about a hundred and asked our grandson to help me. We had almost finished pounding one of them in with a hammer when the plastic cap flew off and struck his face; taken aback, he nevertheless returned to the task next to his sobered grandpa. I took on another job after a visit by an octogenarian, who was a better Methodist than driver. Because the Leyland cypress now leaned to the northwest, I pushed it back upright and bolstered it with a wheelbarrow-load of dirt. Unfazed, it continued to prosper.

Every now and then I strolled among the trees noting where a tiny oak had its own twin trunk that needed to be sacrificed, or where a patch of weeds could hold a sapling, or where some twig bore little glossy orange spheres. Upon an eroding path I spread the lopped-off lower branches of the Christmas tree, which took all winter to fade. Mainly I labored. "I've given myself a promotion," I announced to the carpenters, "from Unskilled to Very Unskilled." Biceps stretched shirt; owner maintained Estate maintained owner.

After a snowfall the mulch resembled a heap shoved aside by a plow, and the conifers drooped under white. I didn't want to take a chance, however small, of letting the branches snap, so I walked around knocking off the new burden for a couple of hours of tough-love. *Whap! Shake!* I even throttled all the white-pine saplings while they were still littler than me. I yanked up the bottom branches to rescue them from invisibility, and (in a kind of synesthesia) could feel all the branches lighten as they darkened. White globules sometimes remained like ornaments. Often I'd shake powder onto myself, and once sent ice-drops flying into my eyes. An old leather coat kept me warm and Greg's red poncho kept me dry, partly exonerating him for breaking his promise to help work at the cabin. Thick gloves, although soaked, protected my hands until darkness and temperature both fell. Some of my finger-and thumb-tips required bandages.

The first autumn a young deer rubbed some kind of velvet off its antlers onto a few transplants, simultaneously rubbing off the bark. To prevent such vandalism the second year, we wrapped black-plastic drainage-pipes around a dozen saplings. The first winter the weeping cypress had reason to bawl after a deer chewed off many of its drooping leaves. But new foliage slowly healed the depredation, and the next winter we sprayed it with noxious repellent and encircled it with a wire fence.

We were becoming rooted and seasoned.

Footnote:
1. Pleasantville, New York: Readers Digest, 1990, p. 180.

5. Snowfallen World

Beyond the frosty storm window of our living room in Illinois, the long, black night had dumped a new dispensation. Sparkling flakes obscured the rotting leaves and lifeless grass, the distinction between yards and pavement, even the imaginary property lines. The expanse was yet unbroken by intaglio, arm-flapping wings. The snow also increased my value as a high school sophomore with muscles and shovel, so when a lady phoned to ask if I would clear her neighbor's driveway so he could get to work, I agreed.

My feet left a sequence of imprints where the sidewalk would be. Because whiteness muffled the few ambient sounds, I could easily hear my own hard breathing and the rubbery jingle of my galoshes. I passed the spot where as a three-or-four-year-old I had first beheld a stain of dog-pee. Occasionally I had to use my shovel as a walking-stick to push off from a drift or keep my balance, yet my thoughts enjoyed no such prop. What should I do? I had several regular customers, three in a row, across the street from the other driveway. Two had been my lawn-mowing regulars, moreover, for several years. Did they not stand first in the queue? Two of them worked in the city and had to get out somehow. Yet none of them had phoned to ask for a timely scrape.

I trudged around the corner thinking about my new account, Mr. Smith, as I'll call him, may have been in his late sixties. Once or twice I had greeted him near his office downtown as I walked or pushed my bike on the sidewalk. A rather portly figure in a dark suit, he accorded me only a gruff and unsmiling syllable. Now my parka seemed to tighten and stiffen. I remembered how other adults would greet me with cheerfulness—neighbors, acquaintances of my parents, parents of my schoolmates, customers for my odd jobs or paper routes….

Did I not deserve respect, not just for being myself, but for serving as tiller of the municipal acreage? It was mine, too, the sidewalks, alleys, ball fields, vacant lots, cemetery, parks, stores, backyards, railroad tracks, the oiled-dust streets near the edge of town, the weedy fields beyond it; swamp and lake skated, trees climbed, a telephone pole shinnied. What about the heat-stroke that forced me into bed with the shade pulled down completely after I tried to cut high grass with a reel lawn mower? The town I even inhaled, from the first waft of winter-surviving vegetation, to the new-mown green under my bicycle tires at the swimming-pool park, to the sour smoke of burning leaves, to the automobile exhaust that vented above the dirty fender-droppings into the dense, pure air.

But no vehicle crawled up or down Hawthorn Blvd. to distract me, no tire-chains sang. I made my way up the middle of the invisible street as I climbed toward the driveways just over the top. On my left inclined the white sidewalk. There my only decision had been when to convert a galoshes-gallop to a belly-flop, and where my sled scuttled inches above the icy snow with a strong assist from gravity. Over the the crest, the street would slope down to Western Ave., then continue flat to Prairie, where my pal Stan would slide open his bedroom window and echo my Tarzan yell.

Now I shifted the long wooden handle to my other glove. Why had none of those familiar customers called? Maybe one would appear at the front door. *Glad to see you!* Surely a businessman needed to reach the train station. Both retired sister-widows could easily remain at home, so perhaps I could dispatch two jobs, cross the street to the requested one, then return.

How could I be so uneasy at a simple trudge uphill? On the way to my piano lesson in the dark, alert for the sound of a horn or the glimmer of a headlight, I would follow the westbound third rail to a long breach, cross that set of tracks, circle eastward on a little path, and cross the eastbound track at another break in its third rail.

Making the conflict worse, I had an eerie sense that Mr. Smith's age, physique, and gray skin made him a candidate for a heart attack. How easy it would be for me to lean into the heavy snow and toss it to the side all the way up to his garage. Yet had he not been distant, had he not jumped the queue? My parka began to rub my neck at the throat-flap. Reaching the crest I surveyed the three houses on the right but perceived no stuck cars, no tire-treads to indicate an exit and a canceled dilemma. Again I remembered looking up at the burgher as he disregarded the gaze of an urchin; again I heard my promise.

After a half-hour of bending, leaning, scraping, lifting, and tossing, I noticed that drops of sweat had sprinkled my shovel. Then I looked up for a moment to behold a revolving light as it made its way up the street and tinged the snow red. That such a momentous vehicle could be silent!

Abandoning the swathe of newly bare cement, I cut across the street to Mr. Smith's porch, where I stood overlooking the partly-shoveled driveway. As two men carried him out on a stretcher, he looked up at me with rheumy eyes as saliva bubbled around his lips. I stood holding my useless blade, looking down at him with sympathy, dread, and guilt, praying that he would not infer even a hint of triumph.

6. Geodyssey III: "Erzerum Coming!"

Despite its metal bars, the third-class-ticket window promised first-class adventure. Amid the rush we found ourselves mingling with some Turkish guys who made sure that the agent regarded our student's discount card (which lowered the price to $5), and that he gave us a ticket to the railhead near the end of the Anatolian Plateau rather to a closer town—a name we couldn't read—and pocketing the difference.

A fellow led us to the train, one of five or six headed by locomotives ready to puff off towards the Mediterranean, Russia, or the East. Through the jammed carriages we labored, knocking our luggage into everything. I got a little discouraged as our expedition into Asia threatened to come without seats. Our new acquaintance haltingly told us that he was trying to make arrangements, and we told him that meanwhile we wouldn't mind sitting temporarily on our sleeping bags in the entryway of a car. We did so. I was beginning to get uncomfortable and bored.

Later on a student came to our little rest area and bade us to follow him. We found ourselves in a compartment bursting with young men. "So crowded," I thought, "but at least we have a seat." We stuffed away our bags and watched all the faces smiling at us and each other. The Turks chatted among themselves in affectionate tones, some of them apparently bidding farewell and about to exit the train. Would I be able to sleep lying down, or would the trip be an endurance contest? I tried to ask how many were staying but got no decipherable response. After a good deal of walking in and out, three students remained in the compartment and waved out the window. Then the platform began sliding backwards.

"Where you live?" asked one of the guys with embarrassment. "Ah- me-di-kah," he repeated after me. It took me a long time to understand that they went to school in Istanbul but were going home for a vacation in Erzerum, near the border of Russia and Iran. "Do you have a ... a dodderling?" No, but I took out my wallet to show him the photo of a pretty classmate. Trying to be a good sport (my mother's ideal), I asked if he had a girl friend. Giggles. As we passed through a village, I noticed strange machines skirting back and forth in the night—not automobiles but horse-drawn cabriolets. "Where you live in Ahmedikah?" My carefully enunciated answer drew a response: "Oh-h-h. Sheekahgo." Animated Turkish chit-chat.

While Tom asked what they studied, I wondered how we'd divide up the sleeping places. My brain was getting foggy as I computed: five fellows plus baggage. If we could lie one-to-a-seat.... "Hey, Tom! Why don't we sleep on the luggage racks?" No response from anyone, and I was afraid to broach any new idea. I sweated out some more chatting.

"You stay Istanbul?" After learning of our three-day sojourn, he gave me a look of "What a shame!" and asked, "You not like Istanbul?" "Oh, man, I gotta sleep," I forbore replying. Tom came through with good words about the city, giving me time to compute. Let's see: five guys ... wow, they got a lotta baggage ... why not recline on those nice long, solid wooden shelves! "... was very beautiful," finished my diplomatic partner. I wondered how to press this idea to Mr. Sleep Anywhere and his buddies.

My notion turned out to be familiar practice, and the Turks were even set to give us the choice rack-beds. I convinced one of the fellows to spread out their baggage while Tom and I stuck our junk all over the compartment. Into some cranny went my leather boots, lent by my younger brother Greg and a size too large. Tom and I had mailed our attaché cases home from Istanbul with our dress clothes and shoes, and with my European journal embellished by autographs of people we'd met.

Now we carried only bedrolls, a large cloth bag of food, knapsacks heavy with clothing fresh and dirty, a small bottle of paregoric, toiletries, a little flashlight, a miniature German dictionary, and a proud passport. I also toted a hardcover book on capital development in poor countries (bought in Oxford and never to be read). A folded, thick-plastic poncho jammed an outer pocket. We each carried a blue plastic folder of American Express checks, strangely thin for such weighty American dollars. Tom shouldered a camera with its leather strap, but his gloves had been stolen at the YMCA in Istanbul. Although apprehensive about the dangers of traveling, we carried no weapon.

Tom suggested that he lie on the floor, as the other guys had no sleeping bags. Filthy and flat is restful compared to the clean, right-angled upright bench that we had occupied through much of Yugoslavia. Wistfully I remembered the first night of our trip, when the two vans parked overnight outside Pittsburgh and we climbed atop sixty institutional-size ping-pong tables for a loftily deep slumber. We passengers all ended up cached in various ways, I content among cigarette butts. (Ironically, half the funds for the trip had come from scrubbing floors, often on my knees, after a best-practice tutorial by one of the widowed sisters, and often with a scrub & buff machine lent by family friend Ellen Dunning.)

Our companions knew Turkish passenger-tricks. Although they couldn't do much about the conductor who "got us" as we were almost asleep to check our tickets, they applied the right verbal formulas to people who kept opening the door, and physical ones to those who barged in. Rails clicked, carriage swayed and shook me to luxuriant nothing.

Vague stirrings, which I ignored. More little noises.... After fewer than six hours, my companions were getting up. A waste of precious restorative time. I looked for solace from

Tom but again seemed to be the odd one. There I lay, human linoleum, with early birds pecking around me. "Why don't you blow a damn trumpet, Tom," I thought as I rolled up my sleeping bag. How could his habit of rising early—engendered by working at his dad's factory before high school classes—have followed him across the ocean? The sun was rising over the plains, turning our dingy compartment an incongruous cheery pink.

Breakfast came out of burlap. A tangy orange, some bread and cheese for me. I mechanically fed myself while staring at the new landscape. Barren. The Turks lazed around in their pajamas while I nibbled chocolate, there being no opium. Now why was it only me that hated a daylong sauna? Enough with the carefree. Every so often I would escape from the Turkish bath to cold storage; and during escapes to the WC, I'd look through the squat-hole at the ties as they blurred back toward Istanbul.

The corridor held little fold-out seats beneath the windows, so whenever someone walked through either way, I'd have to collapse my home. Back to Hot. I hung up my coat and sat in the corner with my precious *Time* magazine, November 1961.

Unable to be civil, I isolated myself from everything but, ironically, the "People" section. Once in a while a Turk ventured a few syllables but I couldn't muster interest. After half an hour, I felt a hand slip my magazine from me. Just take it. The person attached began to flip through it with his friends, examining the advertisements. I stared out the window with my mouth open. Why not put crumbs in my undershirt?

When they inquired about an ad, I couldn't explain it well because of their unfamiliarity with American life and the English language. Finally they laid the thing down on the small fold-out table; I picked it up and retired to my corner and, unable to set my back to them, set it toward Iran.

As the topography swelled, the train searched for the fewest isobars. In the hall I cooled my nose near the plate glass, occasionally rewarded by a vista of the train's entire arc. The locomotive chugged on in the sun and poplars glistened against the blue sky, perhaps drawing a smile.

Then arrived the boy, maybe seven years old, full of pep. Whoever heard of a Turk with blue eyes? As we peered out an aisle window in a vaguely northern direction, he stood on a little ledge so that his head was even with mine and I felt those bright orbs fixed on me. No curiosity, no wonder, fear, or friendliness, just two beams. Was he mentally ill? And there it was in his hand, what I had vaguely feared as a nomad: he aimed it at me, squeezed the trigger, and out came a long squirt.

Once, looking far ahead, I saw that the wheeled-and-rodded boiler was about to enter a tunnel and tried to guess the exact moment we passengers would reach it. *Woomph!* Nothing but darkness, the clacking, the unseen surveillant, "Beat it, kid," I growled later. He finally turned to survey the landscape and I retreated to the compartment, hung up my coat, and took out my chocolate, which to my surprise hadn't melted.

"Hey, Randy," Tom reprimanded me, "all the world knows that tone of voice."

"I *meant* it to be that tone of voice!" Exiting, I plumped down on a board-seat with my hands warming a coat pocket and my breath fogging the air. That afternoon I wanted badly to doze off. But the various benches were taken up, and on one rack lay—dare I reveal the name? My fellow hookey-player slept away, then woke up and lay there and lay there and lay there.

The next day brought the freshness of a decent sleep. The train labored up a slight incline, and as the hours passed, the terrain became more mountainous. Into the first snow we had seen puffed black cinders, and down came the flakes to cover any ugly features of the landscape.

For diversion Tom and I hiked through connecting vestibules to the second class section and then to the first. There I passed Lord Essex, my nickname for a British gentleman I had met on the ferry: his attire rather elegant, he had stood poking the ferrule of a dapper-wrapped umbrella against the deck and keeping his distance from my scruffy forwardness. Tom and I spoke briefly with several young people who were traveling together, one of them a woman, O rare and treasured creature!

The train would sometimes pick up farmers carrying shovels and other tools. These peasants in ragged outfits had tanned, wrinkled faces. One couple got on board with a little girl who seemed apprehensive about that man who was rumpled and even bearded (a rarity at the time). Her parents also had doubts but smiled shyly when the child peeped around them and drew a wink. After watching the snow dance into chasms, I turned around to play peek-a-boo and induce a laugh. The conductor checked our tickets time and again, perhaps from boredom.

Our meals were still emerging magician-like from the sack. Although my chocolate was gone, we still had staples, plus wine—all refreshingly chilled because Tom had thought to hang the larder out the window in a netted bag. We enjoyed sharing vittles with our companions. I loved to say, "Take another piece, go ahead!" and see a fellow smile. After one guy held out an orange and made me take it, another offered his knife to me and made a peeling gesture. Pretending that my orange was frozen, I was unable to puncture the skin with the knife, grimacing "Aargh!" as my companions laughed. Tom opened the window and made as if to hang the bottle outside without the net.

After lunch I might read my magazine, saving the best parts for last. I might re-scan a precious letter from the U.S.A. or take out a book and read a few parts to Tom. We'd wonder about our friends in college—where the sophomore year was carrying on without us—and laugh about good times with our new acquaintances in Europe. We would also wonder about longitudes-to-come:

"Hope we'll be able to get a bus from this place." "Yeah. I sure hope they run regularly in the winter." "Maybe we'd have to take that one train through Russia." I'd pull out my small-scale world atlas, given to us by the steward on our Atlantic voyage, to look over the route again. "Think we'll ever get to this pink one?" "I don't know; it looks like this green one'll never end."

I had used up my magazine asylum, with its mute symbols ordered into words, grammar, and paragraphs. Out the window passed Drab. I sat leaning against the wall in a fog when who should slide open the door of our compartment and tiptoe in—but Miss Winsome, who pressed her small warm pillows against me, caressed my beard, and made intimate offers, even to iron my pants, although I probably had dozed off.

One late afternoon, after two or three days, a compartment mate announced: "Erzerum coming!" Good news because our diet was losing its appeal and I needed to shave the wiry hairs under my chin. I would cut off the whole beard if it would make me less of a curiosity to the blue irises.

"Don't be so intolerant, Randy," said Tom back in the box. "He's a nice little kid if you give him a chance. I get along with him fine. He came in here and started talking to me, so I answered him. We talked a while and had a good time. Of course we couldn't understand each other, but he was real happy." I felt like screaming "OK, Mr. Perfect, why don't you wear your coat in this damn hell of a compartment and pretend it's not hot!" But I just slid open the door and walked out in disgust, although after a few weeks I was able to entertain some admiration.

High spirits returned as once again we began to roll, pack, and tie up. The fridge was reeled in and the wine emptied. "Want this?" "Oh yeah, thanks." "Would you hold down the end of this while I roll it up?" "Sure, which end?" "The one on the end there." As the door slid open, the kid gave us a farewell shot and darted out.

I joined the passengers who stood in the hall and watched for signs of town. The glass momentarily framed a military jeep that both waited at a crossing and slid off-screen to the right, followed by buildings and roads. I began to haul my baggage into the corridor but was prevented by a smiling compartment-mate who gestured in a swinging motion toward the window.

No taxicabs at the station, only sleighs, for whiteness was everywhere and deep. In the dusk this place seemed to be the farthest outpost of Siberia, snow blending with sky but contrasting with buildings and metal runners. Bells tinkled faintly as horses padded along. I hopped off the stairs and felt a strange give under my leather boots. Directly out of compartment came suitcases, bags, and green canvas knapsacks, my job being to keep an eye on the luggage while people went off to check on hotels and buses. Our buddies helped us with everything, even telling the driver where to take us. Boisterous goodbyes. Again I struggled to don my backpack, the familiar yoke of mobility.

Jing jing jing jing.... Tom invited me to sit with the driver while he took the rear seat, which faced backward. Thick, heavy blankets pulled over our laps, we coasted through the white darkness. My companion, turning around with a grin, gestured to the driver that he should lend me the reins.

7. Like A Member of the Family

Near my galoshes in the snow, a puddle of urine. It is all the more vivid because as a little boy—this was soon after The War—I am not looking from far above it. I notice a clash between the yellow, oily blotch and the surrounding whiteness, even between its mysterious luminosity and the gray sky. Lifting my gaze down the roughly-shoveled sidewalk, I behold another dribble in a pile of cast-off snow. The thought comes to me that there might be yet another. So I raise my eyes to a point farther down the grade and do indeed spy one, two, several more. Perhaps these stains forecast my later ambivalence about the animal and its owners (including myself).

In *The Botany of Desire: A Plant's-Eye View of the World*, Michael Pollan notes that the wolf seems more impressive than the dog. "Yet there are fifty million dogs in America today, only ten thousand wolves."

> So what does the dog know about getting along in this world that its wild ancestor doesn't? The big thing the dog knows about—the subject it has mastered in the ten thousand years it has been evolving at our side—is us: our needs and desires, our emotions and values, all of which it has folded into its genes as part of a sophisticated strategy for survival.**(1)**

Through selective breeding, we bipeds shaped an actual creature. Out of the wolf came more breeds than did products from the oleoresin of the longleaf pine. But conversely, the dog defines human beings. It testifies to our affection toward, even admiration for, another species. It records our negligence and occasional cruelty toward our own. And it mutely reports the way we treat it responsibly and irresponsibly.

A small minority of dogs still earn their living as skilled laborers, or as hunters, while many do so as home-alarm systems. Most serve as company. In doing so, they satisfy a human need to close the gap between us and other mammals, even egg-layers. We seem to enjoy recovering a long-lost kinship, of tasting the sap from the Tree of Life.

I myself must pet a certain animal (down the road from the stone angel) even though I'm not sure what it is (photo above).

European-influenced people now tend to regard the dog as more than a cur or a source of protein. In France, it may even warm a restaurant cushion, even cling to the back of a ski. In China people might keep a dog as a pet—but "Not in the house!" exclaimed a waitress as she swept an imaginary critter out. (So not in the bed, a place that about half of American dogs share with their owners.) According the restaurant's placemat, however, anyone born in the Year of the Dog is loyal and honest and works well with people.

Positive or negative—in some regions, the dog is despised—we often invest it with a significance that would not prevail in the courtroom of logic. As always, we tend to follow the Hokey Pokey command to "put your whole self in," whether to anything major or minor: a rectangular piece of fabric with a colorful design, the pronunciation of *caramel*, a few verses in Arabic, the influence of celestial bodies on human ones, ghosts either holy or hair-raising, Beanie Babies, and not to forget the 'Dawgs. Our whole self may even include Rover—as a trotting, panting, wagging, barking ambassador-without-portfolio.

Our species values this animal partly because it's not human. Entertaining, sometimes beautiful, maybe cute (even grotesquely so), it is always trusting and affectionate, at least toward its owner. "I was longing for a woman," reports our countercultural friend Bill, "with hairy legs, love in her eyes, and not much talk—and then my dog crawled up on me and put her front leg over my chest." Soon after another friend's divorce, she reported with amusement how her big dog Ralph would sit in the passenger seat and rest a proprietary foreleg on the window ledge. A dog can "speak," but unlike a human it can't lie, nag, make cutting remarks, or even use a sarcastic tone. It might sulk but can't be snide.

Yet the warm phrase "animal companion" blurs the uniqueness of human ones, with all their complex pleasures and strains. A dog can catch a Frisbee but not a joke. It can't read (so it needn't obey "Keep Dogs Leashed"). Granted, it is at least There, tongue and tail, often very welcome and in fact a blessing for the solitary. A pet also helps owners connect with each other immediately and warmly ("Is that a labradoodle?").

But as for the animal's distinction as "man's best friend"—well, such a pal doesn't lick us or wallow in road-skunk. A true friend (example Tom) stops by your house and walks to high school with you. One Saturday morning stops by and asks if you want to walk twenty miles to Chicago. Or one summer day asks, "When are we going?"—thereby resuscitating an enterprise, collapsed under the weight of its knapsack, by offering to travel with you. Or decades later hands you *The Botany of Desire*.

When does affection warm-puppy into sentimentality? Mr. Bojangles still grieved after thirty years. We give dogs he-and-she pronouns and people-names. Moreover, according to our friend Jane, a single American dog uses more earthly resources than one Ethiopian human.

Indeed, we tend to elevate dogs over humans.

A heroic exception. During World War II a black Siberian husky earned the respect and gratitude of besieged humans. In 1944, snow and fir branches roofed a ditch that sheltered twenty people for eight weeks. Among them was Alzbeta Kačmarova, born in 1928. Bombs exploded all around because the Russians and German armies had converged in Slovakia, the southeastern third of Czechoslovakia. Battles on each side of the Ondova River separated the members of her extended family. A sort of mascot for the ditch-dwellers was Bobi. Once he disappeared for two days, then returned for two more, then went off again. Elizabeth thought, "I bet he has gone to see my parents." She told the story to a group of college students more than sixty years later:

"So I wrote a letter and put it on his neck. I found a black—like this pocketbook—tar paper and I made what looked like a collar. He disappeared and delivered that letter to my mother and my father through the German and Russian front. That thing was full of mines, and we didn't know how he went because two days later he came with the answer from my mother and my father that they were alive. They had had to move to another village because they were too close to the front."

Not only did her parents write, but also General Klapalek, who wanted intelligence on the German occupation.

"They warned us to be very careful because we could get shot. Who cares already [*throws hands in air*]? So I just wrote everything that was on the German side because we used to dig those foxholes every place. So I wrote everything and the dog went with all this information. Two days later he came again with information from the general."

This courier shuttled back and forth three times and gave valuable specifics about the German situation. On the east side the young woman's father—like Ernest Lion's, a decorated veteran of World War I—accompanied the general and told him every place of importance. The Russians destroyed the German occupation and then in a couple of days simply left, whereupon the local survivors moved to what remained of houses.

"All of a sudden this dog came and he was wounded. But he came right to me and started to cry—and I tried to put a bandage on his shoulder—his skin was cracked and hanging. He just turned around, I patted him and talked to him and he went outside. And I never saw him again. He knew it wasn't what it used to be."**(2)**

In the postwar years, dogs shared the author's childhood, as they did many a person. An eight-year-old on a trip to the West Coast, I beheld my first Saint Bernard at the Mt. Rainier Lodge and immediately fell upon its bulk with a hug, a sensation that I still recall fondly. On television Buster Brown's dog Tige lived in a leather residence. During one film, a collie was the first to learn from Edmund Gwenn that the mistress had died. In *Uncle Wiggly's Happy Days*, by Howard R. Garis, the circus clown dog kept barking "Hurry! Hurry! Hurry!" even after his abandonment by the rest of the troupe (like a scene from the Theatre of the Absurd).**(3)** Little black and white Scotty-magnets repelled each other.

In our neighborhood I felt a kinship with four-legged Stupe because both of us were neighborhood criss-crossers. Patiently affectionate, he would allow me to pat his flank, and I can still feel his black curls and hear the hollow whump-whump. After reading how to approach a dog—slowly, with the back of the hand extended downward to allow the animal a sniff—I did so many times, often feeling warm breath and wet nose.

But since pets could run free, feces abounded in various stages of dissolution, including mysterious white turds, perhaps of ghost animals. My brothers and I caught pinworms, no doubt from playing in the contaminated grass—the tickles themselves then cavorting in the gut—so we had to get enemas and take gentian violet. When my brother Cap choked on one of these pills, my father had to haul him upside down and whap his back to dislodge it.

As a boy I heard my mother announce that somebody had poisoned a neighbor's dog. I was incredulous. "Why?!" She quit stirring the pudding, thought for a moment, and explained that the animal might have plagued someone by digging up a garden or barking. Yet I could not absorb such news. I did not yet understand that to some people *Mi perro es su perro*. "I love my Jack Russell" on the rear windshield is *mi*; Jack on the lap of the distracted driver is *su*. "There it goes again," declared my mother in exasperation. I looked out the kitchen window to the flower garden, where an alien beast was dragging itself along. "Its back legs are paralyzed and they won't put it to sleep."

One next-door neighbor had a dog called Nicky, whose coat disturbed me with its mysteriously bare, pink, scabby places. But the other adjoining neighbors had a dog that provided my first job: while they were visiting their daughter in California, I went down the basement every day, fed the animal, and scraped up its piles with a shovel. A dozen years later, in the summer of 1962, I passed a day indoors with Stupe, whose owners were reluctant to leave it alone in case of a house fire. This concern benefited more than my wallet, for while old Curly Hair napped all afternoon, I fashioned a scrapbook of business cards and pen-and-ink sketches that recorded a multi-month expedition.

My pal down the street had a short, stiff-legged dog. The cute name Bootsie seemed incongruous because every time I visited, the animal had to be collared and restrained behind the kitchen door, which it scratched madly while trying to get a slippery purchase on the linoleum. At this reaction I felt a disturbed wonder, unable to form the concept *gratuitous paroxysm of hostility.* Yet my friend cared enough for this pet that, when we took a jaunt out of town, he ducked into a butcher shop, asked for a bundle of bloody, cast-off bones, and stood holding them in the vestibule of the train.

Over on Hawthorn Blvd., Stan's boxer would rush the back door as it opened in a snorting, snout-frothing frenzy. "Sandy is out!" his mother would cry in despair, and we would run around the yard trying to catch it. My own family got a cocker spaniel with an ill-suited name, Creampuff, who bit a policeman to death (the dog's). Our next pet was given to us by someone who evidently considered an elegant Gordon Setter a hot potato. From it I learned that a pet can require sacrifice:

"Whose dog is that?" I turned to peer over the back of the hay-wagon and saw Luke, who had followed me a half mile. The wizened farmer, holding the reins to a pair of horses, said, "He'll nip the horses. You gotta take him back." I jumped out from among the other sixth-graders and ran down Linden to where it ended at Kenilworth across from Tommy Hollinger's house. Leaning to the left, I raced south past Hawthorn to Cottage, then turned left again and secured the animal in our yard. Sprinting back to Linden I found vacant pavement.

Remembering that the wagons or sleighs went north, I put my tennis shoes to work again, ran back to Kenilworth, turned right, and continued past Linden to Elm. I knew that the rides either turned right onto that street or rolled to the countryside, then turned right on St. Charles Road. If only it was a sleigh so I could follow its tracks! Not seeing the wagon, I continued running north for fifteen minutes, almost to St. Charles, but spotted nothing 'way past the few houses along it, so I began cutting through the country backyards and running parallel to the road eastward. In good shape after mowing, walking, or biking around town, I nevertheless had to stop to catch my breath and tend to a pain in my side. I continued to jump over weeds and to dodge trees, bushes, leaf-piles, and laundry-line poles, always keeping an eye out for a glimpse of my jam-packed, laughing schoolmates.

Finally I reached Western, where I turned right, now hobbling. Bent over a knife in my gut, I sat on the curb. My mind echoed with a mocking *clip-clop, clip-clop*. After a while I managed to stand up and make my way down the sidewalk to Hawthorn, then turned right, and limped up the slope and over the crest toward home.

A dozen years later, downtown in Wyoming, my roommate urged me to turn around, and I met the gaze of a half-cocker spaniel in a pet-store. Only the plate glass kept us from leaping into each other's arms. But every workday I had to leave Huey indoors, and once I returned to a television lying cracked on its side next to my roommate's fractured, extra-tall bottle of wine. On the dog's evening walk, it would make a shuddering deposit on the parkway. (Who has not polished a shoe with Fidola? Once I stepped out of our motor home, vehicle of choice for dog-owners, and just missed a brown cairn, one of innumerable such piles that mark a trail all over the world.) During another walk I saw the animal bolt into an intersection and almost get run over, so when I was able to breathe again I gave it away. Yet when a collarless dog appeared at the door trembling and sneezing, I provided a box-bed inside for several days. It returned immeasurable gratitude as a terrible cold.

Then in North Carolina "Whitey" (as I called him) used to follow me as I walked to the university, petted him, and enjoyed his nearby trotting. One day he darted into a spinning hubcap, bounced off, and ran away. The owner declined to believe my report, and the dog or its shade materialized sometime later. Another time I was riding up that same hill in a friend's car, a Saint Bernard bolted away with its leash and crashed into the right front wheel. Although stunned, it was apparently unhurt, but the owners angrily berated the driver.

A woman in our apartment complex loved her pet, and once when she dressed it in a hat and maybe a scarf, we shared a laugh. But sometimes when I walked to the hill, the dog came after me with head lowered and teeth bared. After I complained, the animal was tethered—but then came after me dragging its rope-and-stake. After I had clapped it away on two occasions, feeling the hair on my arms rise, I called the police, and the dog disappeared. The woman started telephoning me and yelling "Bastard!" before hanging up. This practice stopped only with the intervention of the law and the phone company.

One day in an elevator I complained to someone about how owners tended to value their dogs over people. Her face hardened. She thought for a moment and declared, "If my dog and a person were both drowning, I don't know which one I would save." The door opened and out she huffed. Grateful for my ability to swim, I was nevertheless shocked. In retrospect I find her reaction ironic, for as an African American her ancestors were considered lower than humans and listed as possessions along with animals.(4)

When we first tried to settle in a South Carolina town, things began inauspiciously when a neighbor asked if I had seen his black Lab. No, sorry. "I've seen you petting it. They'll follow you if you pet 'em. That's bad dog-etikwette."

A friend from Mississippi gave Marge that beautiful cocker spaniel puppy. Once as I swam in the river near our house, the animal couldn't restrain her affection and jumped off the pier and paddled toward me. During thunderstorms I would hug its trembles, and we would play yank-the-rag as both of us went *grrr-r* and the whites of her eyes threatened fierce things. "She was always there whenever I came back from taking call at night," Marge remembers fondly. The turf-conscious dog, however, did not welcome everyone. A young man rang our doorbell and angrily reported that the animal had scared his little brother by running up at him and barking. I apologized and asserted that she was harmless. Although I couldn't, or wouldn't, fully appreciate the boy's distress, I later acknowledged Moonbeam's streak of Bootsie.

That Wyoming stray seemed to track me down after a decade. Rangy, thin, collarless, it wandered up and down the South Carolina road and around the yards while the resident canines made a fracas. A few wags of its tail, however, called forth some pieces of bread along with the assumption that the creature would move on. After the food disappeared as a momentary bulge in its throat, I coaxed it to me, patted it, and spoke a few words. Next morning the dog lay curled on my front porch. I tried to appear unfriendly and after the squatter had remained a few hours gruffly commanded it to "Get movin'!"—only to see the tail swing back and forth. As Sa'di wrote, "A dog will never forget the crumb thou gavest him, though thou mayst afterwards throw a hundred stones at his head."

I took the cocker for a walk every day, when the animal's golden hair would fluff in the breeze as it ran through lawn and field searching for adventure with its nose. But this time the stray came along and followed at my pace while the thoroughbred meandered about us. The interloper had to sit down every now and then to take its back claws repeatedly to its flank, a self-prescribed treatment for an advanced case of mange.

From that time on, I feared for Moonbeam. Alternatives: tolerate the stray and risk an expensive, maybe futile, treatment for my own pet; lay out money to try curing someone else's animal; or keep the trespasser away. Ashamed of my contradictory messages, I began to stomp, clap, and yell. But the dog appeared to have settled upon its last chance. One day I shook a rock in a big can to scare it, but when the clatter stopped, back it drifted, although remaining at a distance. The animal seemed unconscious of me only during a scratching spell: no longer of this world, it would twist awkwardly and claw away at its thin torso. This beast I both pitied and detested. "You ask too much. There are too many dogs around here already, and no one else will take you in either. Why can't you just trot on and suffer elsewhere, maybe get out of your misery by a speeding car? How do you think I feel about denying comfort to the mistreated?" *Scratch, scratch, scratch.*

About this time I threw the can at him and wondered where he got the energy to run. Then he slunk back, head abased, eyes cast up humbly and furtively, tail wagging tentatively. The mutt now actually seemed to smile, as if to apologize for its own role: "I know I'm ugly and beset with disease, and have nothing to offer. I can't demand a thing. You're the one, that's all. I'm sorry it's come to this and I don't hold anything against you. We must play our parts."

Embarrassed about throwing things and unhappy about the friendly tail and the mange-germs on the front mat, I called the police. The car arrived with its official label and trunk, which the man opened. When he expressed concern lest the dog bite, I replied almost defensively, "No, no!" The officer held up the core of an apple that he'd been munching and coaxed the animal to the bumper. I then put my arms around its patchy fur and, straining, lifted him into the trunk as he gingerly took the core. Apprehensive, he was nevertheless settled into the hold and the lid was shut with care. As the light narrowed and disappeared, the captive, holding the fruit in its mouth, lost any vestige of innocence.

After I complained about a next-door neighbors' noisy dog, they gave me a tour of piles on their side of the fence, so I kept our pet tied to an elevated wire near a comfy doghouse.

Sometimes, however, I let it run loose when I was around. One night a few shrieks drew me to the side of the little-traveled road, where the animal lay. As I felt its warm flank, the last bit of life widdled out. I had to give the news to a tearful Marge, then as further punishment shovel out a hole under the pine needles. *Whose dog was that?*

The mouth of Man's Best Friend is filled with forty-two reminders of its ancestor.

In 1943, a year before the courier Bobi undertook his missions, Ernest Lion and his new wife climbed out of the train-prison to the platform at Auschwitz. They were surrounded by SS military with pointed machine guns: "German shepherd dogs were at the ready to attack, flashing their fangs and leaning hard into the leashes."**(5)** In *The Pilgrim's Progress*, by John Bunyon (Part I, 1678), a great barking dog scares the women and children as they approach the allegorical gate of prayer. "Nor durst they for a while dare to knock any more, for fear the mastiff [i.e., the Devil] should fly upon them."

Back in the hometown neighborhood, Greg leaned over a neighbor's dachshund, Nipper, and arose with a punctured, swollen, black-and-blue cheek that provoked a small lawsuit. Once while running along the sidewalk at the corner of Hawthorn and Western, I felt a sharp pain in my leg, stopped, and recognized a snout through the wide-gapped wooden fence. Soon muzzled.

Each spring I took grade-schooler Andrea with me to peddle brooms for the Lions Club. One evening when a front door opened, a heavy dog crashed open the screen door and rammed into her. Upon leaving I heard a plaintive "He *bit* me." The owner, a physician, apologized and examined her stomach then and the next day in his office, finding no serious damage (but overlooking permanent fear). While our family lived in France, eight-year-old Katie returned from that weekend train-trip to Lyon with a bruised cheek and a scabbed lip, the cut the same width as a dog's nail, the scar almost disappearing after years.

As an adult my pal with the manic-scrambling boxer was less fortunate. He was riding a speed-bike downhill when two dogs ambushed him from behind a hedgerow. One of them caused him to tumble over the handlebars to the trauma ward, where he spent two weeks. A rib had punctured a lung, which hemorrhaged profusely and thus required forty full-plate X-rays. He suffered a life-threatening concussion even with a helmet, and the blow from the pavement crushed his shoulder blade to a degree that the orthopedic surgeon had seen only on deceased patients. He had to pay the bills for twenty-two physicians.

If a dog barks and the owner doesn't hear it, does it make a sound?

Barking is acoustic poop. It's a negative externality—i.e., something that originates on one property to the detriment of another—such as an eight-foot-high wooden cross decorated with plastic roses, spot-lit at night, and attended by a cement angel. Noise can blight the soundscape. It can even emanate from a hotel room while the owners are dining out, so that someone else has to change rooms; or while they eat breakfast and leave other patrons in the kennel.

In television documentaries by Ken Burns, the camera slow-pans over a photograph of yesteryear's town to a faraway, dubbed-in barking. But many a living citizen must contend with a four-legged larynx. Granted, Bowser can warn of a dangerous trespasser, but more likely the culprit is a squirrel, a delivery truck, a neighbor trimming bushes, or another dog. So the pet is the thief. As for the range and quality of its vocalization—envy the deaf. "I had rather hear my dog bark at a crow," says Beatrice to Benedick, "than a man swear he loves me" (*Much Ado*, I.1). Such noise is hard to ignore, like a baby's squall (self-preserving rhetoric), a leaf-blower (sound-blasting paint off the neighborhood), a boom-box (Irrational Public Radio), or its cousin the decibellied motorcycle.

The motto of a magazine called *Bark*: "My dog is my co-pilot." Because of such hairy aviators, our friends the Roes sold their house in suburban California. Ralph nicknamed each one:

Yipper (house on left): rat terrier, high pitched yips.

Yapper: small Pomeranian, medium-pitch yaps.

Yelper: medium dog, low-pitch normal barks. This trio loved to stand on top of sofa next to picture window, watching for any person walking by to bark at. The rat-dog would jump up and down while barking. Unceasing, even when the owners and their teenage kids were at home, which I never understood. The barking hurt my ears even when the dogs were inside and the windows closed.

Barbara Boxer (house behind): boxer, barked less but a large dog with a lower pitch.

Joe Boxer, her twin. They would jump up on a garden bench, then stretch to look over the fence whenever I was working in my yard. They stopped barking when I talked to them. Hard to focus on gardening. Would bark when I went back inside.

Woofer 1 (house on right): dark brown Rottweiler with a deep, menacing bark, and a mean look.

Woofer 2: ditto. This one would eye me as if he were thinking of lunch.

Surround 1 (house behind previous house): mystery dog that I never saw, but he would always bark after the Rottweilers wound up (like an echo).

The Roes checked out an acre for sale in Virginia by stomping around and making noise. They now enjoy "hearing only the faint sounds from a donkey, horses, goats, and cows."**(6)**

As a young man, my friend from Michigan would visit a girl and sleep with her on the living room floor. But a dog would bark and bark and bark.

> I made friends with it—fed it. One evening, late, I got ahold of the dog, put in my car, and drove it to the park five miles away. I left it there, drove back, thinking I would have a good night's sleep. But by morning the dog woke me up barking again.
>
> It wasn't two weeks later when the dog ran out in front of him and got run over. "I felt really bad." Years later and elsewhere, the dog next door barked a lot. "I walked into the garage one day and it came running in, so I asked, 'Wanna get into the car?' It thought it was goin' for a ride. We did. I took it to the other side of I-96. It found its way back."

Why do dogs bark so inanely? According to *How Come? Planet Earth,* animals become more cub-like and babyish when they are bred to be more docile—foxes, for example. Scientists think that's what happened naturally to wolf-dogs, who were rewarded for being agreeable. Adult wolves rarely bark, and just on business.**(7)**

As early as the eighth grade I first became aware of such an adult puppy. It was a tiny, long-haired breed (call it a Yapillion) that our widowed friend next door would put outside in the evening. One night as I tried to fall asleep so I could rise early for my morning paper route, the constant, high-pitched reports drove me crazy. I ran outside in my pajamas as if to strangle the animal but settled for an in-the-snout *"Shut up!"* Years later Marge and I, about to leave Illinois for North Carolina, had no choice but to listen to a German shepherd rip into the ear of night. So I finally called the police, whereupon a drunken woman phoned to predict that something bad would happen to me before I moved (an after-the-fact prophecy).

In our first South Carolina house the next-door neighbors kept their dog outside, where it frequently barked while they worked all day. By temperament I need quiet, not to pray but to read, write, and think, for my idea of perdition is a room with a television going. When I asked our neighbors to do something about the problem, and noted that the dog had no cover from the rain—for some reason the noise stopped, and my gratitude endures.

But such cooperation is as rare as an alarm clock on the Appalachian Trail. One of our carpenters here in Virginia reported this conversation with her friend, an otherwise admirable person. "Why don't you leave your barking dogs inside while you work? They disturb the whole neighborhood." "I don't care."

Our Virginia house had a neighboring beagle (sounds like bugle). "Trouble brewing," to apply the caption of Gary Larsen's cartoon of the dingo farm next to the daycare. Once I saw the dog carrying a bag of fast-food chicken in its jaws, ran after it, and yanked the leftover bones safely away, but my concern left the owner unmoved. When I complained about the animal's nocturnal serenade, I learned that it's a dog's nature to bark. One night I tied a note on the pet's collar reminding it why I had stamped down our walk the previous night waving a broom. This missive provoked the wrath of a fine and successful person, who swore that he'd get rid of the damn animal if it wasn't for his children. Nevertheless, to the family's credit, the dog was thereafter confined to night-quarters on the opposite side of their house.

A Carolina neighbor moved in with hunting dogs that not only crooned but dug under their cage and ran about tearing up our yard. Complaints were vain. Andrea remembers how the owner, perhaps beered up, once pounded on our front door and scared her: "I'm glad you didn't let him in." The second policeman to answer a call hoped the "n-dogs" had not motivated our For Sale sign.

They largely had. After we'd built another house, moved, and enjoyed a few years amid Southern pines, maples, bays, great-flowering Gordonias (*Gordonia lasianthus,* loblolly bay) and overhead-hanging blueberry bushes, a new neighbor unloaded four or five companions.

The large ebony one would charge with fangs as if to rip the chain-link fence, so I had to avoid that area of the yard. Although the owner claimed to hate barking, these held forth often. In nice weather they forced me to close the tentatively-opened window or go back inside from the screened porch. I hung a detector that beeped shrilly when the pack barked close to the fence; this immediate punishment helped until lightning caused the machine to beep for a couple of hours. I took the broken thing down, a double waste of money since it had required a new electric outlet. Our magistrate explained that the situation did not fall under her purview because it didn't allow an arrest. After a few years, one of the dogs died, according to the notice of decease hanging from the street-side mailbox.

This owner once expressed fear that a third neighbor's animal would cause her a nervous breakdown. Before they had moved in, Marge warned this couple that I could not tolerate a barking dog, but they seemed unimpressed. One Sunday morning I wrote a note, stuck it on their mailbox, and took my anger on a long hike. The woman deemed my letter "nasty." I had indeed called their pet "Sparky" after an eponymous tourist trap with its eyepatch-Dalmation billboard and its orange-and-chartreuse fluorescence. We attempted a rapprochement. They reminded me that when the previous owners told them I detested the bug-zapper, they had removed the industrial-quality Orville Redenpopper.

But the percussions continued even after two visits from the animal control officer. Several complaints did persuade the owners to put a little box on the animal's collar that would emit a tiny shock at a bark, but the effort was occasional and they ended up not following through. Dog was too old, etc. They invited Marge to put the offender in their laundry room if it had a spell while they were gone, and she did so once, but the offer was never repeated for reasons we could only enjoy guessing. Often the owners had to spend the weekend on family missions and left the dog to croon "O Solo Mio." I purchased a second-hand videotape camera, and while Greg was visiting, he and I filmed the show over the fence and mailed the tape around the corner.

One night I frantically drove to a convenience store for a massive bar of chocolate, intending to sicken the animal enough to warn the owners. I unwrapped the plank to avoid a crinkling sound and a shiny reflection, crept between our backyards (staying out of the light cast from a pole), and tossed it 'way over the fence. Next day the mechanical noise resumed. I was unwilling to shoot the beast, as more than one person urged—although my beagle-plagued colleague warned me not to do it after researching the law. Certainly no painful antifreeze or ground glass. Finally, another night I tossed the insomniac a ball of hamburger laced with a few half-hearted sleeping pills. But if the dog died, the bark lived on, to my relief and despair. I ended up pounding a For Sale sign into erstwhile Eden.

As humans continue to domesticate the wolf, it becomes "manifold and divided" (Thomas Aquinas), so far into almost 170 breeds. As for mutts, count the legs and divide by four. Over the last ten millennia of earth-turning, the dog has also revealed a broad range of human behavior. Perhaps Canis Major aims a skeptical Sirius upon the earth.

Author with drinking buddy, 2010.
Photo by Aaron Grady-Brown.

Footnotes:

1. New York: Random House Trade Paperback, 2001, pp. xvi-xvii. Compare the dæmon of Philip Pullman's trilogy, *His Dark Materials*. Often taking the form of an animal, it makes up part of every human, to whom it has a metaphysical connection. But a dæmon possesses human intelligence, speaks, and enjoys independence. "Dæmon: His Dark Materials," *Wikipedia*.

2. Elizabeth K. Pisanchik Moehringer, English 459, 2008. The DVD recording of this talk and the author's edition of the transcript are housed at Coastal Carolina University.

3. Illustrated by Aldren Auld Watson. New York: Platt & Munk, 1947, pp. 17-21.

4. Bequeathed to a son: "one Negro man by the name of Harry—& also one mare & two cows & calves and one bed and furniture." Will of Arthur Alford of South Carolina Horry District 1827. www.hchsonline.org/wills.

5. *The Fountain at the Crossroad*, p. 41.

6. Personal communication, 2011. For a poem on a neighbor's dog as soloist, see Billy Collins, "Another Reason Why I Don't Keep A Gun in the House," www.poemhunter.com.

7. By Kathy Wollard. Illustrated by Debra Solomon. New York: Workman, 1999, p. 134.

8. The Estate II: Snouts & Louts

Marjory and I came home from a party at dusk, which in late May seemed unhurried, even reluctant to disappear over the western horizon. Climbing out of the passenger's seat, I decided to work off some alco-calories by raking up more stones from the field to be sown with clover for bees. Having donned work clothes and boots, I grabbed the handles of the wheelbarrow, which carried the familiar rake, shovel, and rubber basket, and turned it around toward the front of the carport. Above and behind the Subaru—was that a shape? It resolved into something elongated and animated—like the snout of a horse.

Was it not bobbing along with several other equine heads, mainly dark-colored, one of the animals a brown and white paint? This phantasmagoria shuffled and breathed. The beasts made a side-view tableau as if they'd migrated from the galloping Roper shirt I had bought at the Floyd Country Store. Already a bit dizzy, I feared that I was hallucinating and skeptically remembered a wine called "La Linda." To make things worse—was the fourth creature an amalgamation of long-haired bison, black sheep, and mastiff?

Afraid that the sixteen legs would amble down Annie Lane a quarter mile to the highway, I phoned 911 and asked for an officer to mark the intersection with a blue light. Then I ran upstairs and to get two apples and cut them into parts. By then the group had moved farther up the lane toward the woods. Flashlight in hand, I assured myself that although I might be weaving a little in the wheel-tracks, I was dealing with fact. I approached slowly, murmured sweet nothings, held out a quarter of a Red Delicious, caught a large brown eye, and persuaded the scrutinizer to reach out, test, and gobble. The others crowded around me and took shares, the largest pushing away competition, shoving me, and taking an extra slice. I was amazed by their graceful musculature, the sheen of their coats, and their long, costume-like fringes. The stunted one hung back like an abject slave, so I invited it to take a piece, which it half-heartedly dropped on the ground and thus into another mouth.

I was taken back by the height of the other animals—in fact had to tilt my head back to look into the eyes of the biggest—and by the warmth of their breath as it came down upon me. But the thought of teeth and hooves kept me on guard as I moved among them talking, patting noses and flanks, trying to bide time so as to keep them from atop the ridge. I noted that they valued apples more than affection. Still influenced by the meretricious Linda, I confused this group with The Bremen Town Musicians—donkey, dog, cat, and rooster.

By then Marjory had come out of the house with long carrots broken in half, and the quartet clopped back down the lane toward her. Katie soon brought out a second course. Then Marge held out her arms and commanded something like "Don't go any further!" but the visitors just passed around them and took off into the woods. By the time I got there, no animals, just continual barking by several invisible neighborhood sources.

Afraid for the safety of both herd and people, I started to walk down to Rt. 221 with the idea of—I guess shining the light at oncoming cars to warn drivers. On the gravel I spied a line of eight little piles that, already a bit dried, seemed to mark the original path of the escapees and to offer more evidence of reality. I followed the turns that a GPS demarcates as S, SW, S, SW, E, NE, E, SE, SW. Nothing at the bottom of the hill, just an occasional whizzing car. I waved a beam at one driver to warn of hooves loping around the curve by Margie Keith's house.

Trudging back up the hill, I heard an engine and turned to see headlights that approached slowly. As the truck drew next to me, I read "Animal Control." The driver, Scott, knew that the animals had pushed open the gate while their owners were out of town. Having parked, the rescuers kept a few inviting bulbs on and explored the area with a spotlight. My report: "When I saw the Shetland, I vowed to stop drinking."

Kate and I made a second fruitless expedition to the bottom of the hill, then climbed uphill and went indoors.

"Horse!" Marge had been looking out the kitchen window, where the lights of the vehicle illuminated an animal that was tall, powerful, but restrained. I walked down to talk with the genial captor, who had attached the animal to the truck. "He's the leader—the rest will come to wherever he is." Climbing back to the house, I returned with two Granny Smiths. "They like apples," said Scott; "Hold your hand flat." "He'll be your friend forever," added his wife. "They're organic," I assured everyone. A warm breath from above charmed me but a startlingly loud whinny next to my ear caused a backward stumble.

Now the full group had mustered. Scott explained that the dark brown one was a bay (a color that Stewball the racehorse was not). The pony, he added, knew its place, which was at a respectful distance, although this time it did accept a portion of glossy Grandma. Then the headlights of another vehicle slowly made their way up, and from it emerged two friendly and grateful people who knew bridles.

The next morning I peered out the kitchen window across Annie Lane, across the trees and the invisible highway to the hill opposite, where a brown-and-white horse grazed tranquilly in the meadow. Later I started to work in the yard when I spied a large plop near the garden. I shoveled it up—breaking it in half to reveal an interior of something like algae—and carried it sideways and downwind to a hole left by a rock, which I stuffed with souvenir.

The hillside pasture far across Dodd Creek nourished the eye. But one day cattle hooves turned to wheels and silence to cylinders. The mechanical clamor ran up the hill from a natural amphitheater and echoed against houses. A single four-wheeler was eventually joined by other Acoustic Terrorism Vehicles. Around and around they circled unmuffled, and I think they jumped over some kind of ramp. The raw sound could not be shut out, unlike cold, heat, or wind.

The county had scrapped its noise ordinance as unenforceable after a man complained that his neighbor-dog's bark was driving him crazy. (Compare the library that shut its doors because too many people were taking out books.) In legal contrast, the County of Boulder declares that "the peace, health, safety and welfare of its citizens require protection from excessive, unnecessary and unreasonable noise." As Fred wrote:

> Quietude is a prerequisite to clarity of mind and soul. We claim it as a right yet we can deny it so easily to our neighbors by our indifference. Like smoke from a careless fire, noise passes unimpeded across property lines. We can close our eyes, but we can't close our ears." (*Floyd Press*, 17 June 2010.)

And as Tom declared: "Yes, it's your own property, but keep everything on it."

Almost shaking from nerves, I was sustained by the possibility of making an offer on the racetrack and thus buying silence. One night the police, called just before midnight, arrived with their own wheels, and a row of taillights slowly ascended the hill. I visited the Sheriff's Office and learned that officers would help at any time and (apparently) serve as an informal noise ordinance.

The invasion returned on unpredictable days and continued into the evening. The decibels penetrated everywhere in the house from basement to upstairs bedroom on the opposite side. I imagined stringing wires across the path of the ATVs but, not religious, couldn't pray for a lightning bolt.

Once as I walked down noise-racked Annie Lane with Andrea, I explained loudly that we might put the cabin up for sale, and she wept. But why would anyone buy acoustic skunk? Our neighbors drove around the area, heard the racket a mile away, and counseled trying to wait things out. I began to have stomach trouble. Meanwhile the fragile riparian land was now plowed by tires and the air polluted by exhaust.

As time went on, the charging around seemed to become less frequent, and it eventually stopped. Racetrack faded somewhat into pasture, and silence fell like rain after drought. But the scenery would always be provisional. A few times when we heard what turned out to be a chain saw, we flinched.

9. Private vs. Public: Don't Pass, You Pass

"I don't know who the *hell* you are, but this is private property."

Despite the No Trespassing sign, I was hiking along an unpaved road when I detected the sound of pistons and tires behind me. I kept striding along with feigned unconcern in hopes that the vehicle would keep going, but it came to a halt. Down from the open window of a big pickup, a tanned leather face glared through sunglasses. I had no principles to stand on, just this land that was clearly demarcated at the junction of a county road and a firing range.

I apologized and lamely reported that at least I had turned around at the second sign above the ranch itself. "This whole thing is private property." A relief not to be peering down a rifle barrel and risking Cool Hand Luke's failure to communicate. Would this guy call the authorities? Would he spy the dried-up pod I had yanked from his locust tree and stuck in my pocket? It was a souvenir of Colorado for my grandson, who had picked one like it on our retirement acreage in Virginia.

Off drove the Truck of Justice. I felt relieved but stripped of dignity and degrees. Yes, I had broken the law, but how dangerous could a person be who wears fuzzy, pajama-pseudo-camouflage pants (which had drawn the mirth of Katie the graduate student). The driveway of the jolly rancher, moreover, was as wide as a two-lane, and it stretched flat and straight on the near-desert of Boulder County. Why couldn't he have said, "Glad to see you enjoying our road, brother, but can you tell me what's up?"

Mortified, feeling ambivalent about the close-call pod, I walked back to our daughter's house. What should come to mind but the Cyclops tribe in The Odyssey, with their symbolic monovision. "They have no laws nor assemblies of the people, but live in caves on the tops of high mountains; each is lord and master in his family, and they take no account of their neighbors." And I thought of the protagonist in Leo Tolstoy's story "How Much Land Does a Man Need?" (1886); he answered the title's question by trying to claim as many hectares as he could span in a day's run, only to collapse and fill a grave.

I remembered the cyclist that morning in Boulder who yelled "Get out of the way!" for letting my car stand in what I immediately recognized as a bike lane. So in one day I had been rebuked first for treating public space like private, then the reverse.

The realization hit me that I myself had once become public property, and in Colorado.

On July 31, 1967, Selective Service number 11 122 42 91 climbed into a bus full of young men and rode from Wyoming to Denver for a draft physical. This was the first of my travels to be coerced. Even my little house-trailer in Connecticut had served as a kind of trolley, with front and back doors on one side that carried me to a master's degree.

I did not take it amiss when a doctor's fingers checked my privates. Indeed, only a few people in the world made me burn with resentment. One was a stocky haberdasher in Skopje, Yugoslavia, who watched me standing near the mystic yellow light of a Grundig radio and listening in rapture to what was probably Bach. Granted, I wore muddy boots because Tom and I had just hustled through fields to escape from brief captivity after photographing a tank. With a frown, the owner stalked over and poked the Off button, leaving me amid a jumble of shirts and the disorder of travel. But now at the examination center I came to detest several functionaries.

First we underwear-clad candidates enter the big waiting room nervously, some wordless, some jabbering. "Keep it down in here!" An optometrist has charged in: "I can't do this with all this noise!" As more men file out toward the offices, others dribble in, some laughing and talking. In bursts the optometrist again and surprises the newcomers: "The next one who makes noise will be the last one in this whole group to be seen!" Then an awkward fellow lopes in seeks comfort from his own voice. Each of us guards his own butt in silence, not having developed much camaraderie. "You there!" The reappearing eye-guy aims an index finger at the half-naked fellow. "Sit down!" The recruit stares through glasses in humiliation. "You wait till the end of the line!"

Then at the next station I hand the doctor a two-page history of my lumbar problem. "We'll have to have more than *this*," he grunts after scanning a note from my physician. In rapidly failing spirits I submit to an examination and an X-ray. Then I sit in the hall to learn whether I will teach or march. Will I go into basic training a couple of years after the freshmen across the hall, who perhaps flunked out after turning poker cards instead of pages and keeping me awake? Will I throw away the graduate degree funded partly by weekend dishwashing so as to "serve" the country that was yanking me around? College teachers were not being called up; draft them, draft me. Somebody hands me an official-looking slip of paper, which I search for a verdict. Weakly I ask an official what it says. "Can't you read that?!" he snarls, his index finger jabbing the slip; "*You pass.*"

In despair I find my way to the recruiter for O.C.S. and Plan B. I stand there bedraggled as he leans back on the chair with feet on the desk, chatting on the telephone without deigning to look at me. In those days I still admired the late President Kennedy's vow to "bear any burden, pay any price"; still clung to the paradigm of The War, which assumed that war was necessary and righteous. But decades later I see this officer's demeanor as symptom and symbol of the arrogance and even corruption that tinged the whole Southeast Asia debacle—even from its pretext of a beginning.**(1)** After a speech by General Maxwell Taylor, someone asked, "What if the United States just continued to bomb and bomb North Viet Nam until nobody was left?" "Crime doesn't pay," he answered.

After months of appealing the 1-A card, I learned the reason for it: the Selective Service had no record of my handwritten request for deferment. As a compromise, I think, the board let me teach one semester while drafted, with the condition "Postponed," and the next semester another such announcement was taped to the window of my front door (as if to occlude any other prospect). Dare I hope for a full reprieve after I turned twenty-six? Indeed, near the end of the academic year I opened the mailbox to find a 2-A card: Deferred because of civilian occupation.

Countless men have received a draft notice, as in "Die Postkarte," by Heinrich Böll **(2)** and countless have volunteered. Sometimes it has been their parents who received an official message. My great-grandmother Sophia Capps must have held the "Regret to inform you" with the same hand that, fragile and age-spotted, reached over the quilt to touch mine thirty years later, in the late 1940s. Although as an infant she had been carried safely through the smoke of the Great Chicago Fire of 1873, her son "fell" in the Great War.

In the next world war, an Italian bullet grazed the scalp of one soldier, William S. Dunning; had it bitten more deeply I would never have attended his alma mater, Maryville College (an overnight bus journey to Tennessee). There, as a freshman I would talk with children of missionaries and dream up an excursion to Asia—still feasible in the waning *Pax pre-'Nam.*

Ironically my own combat was with my fellow citizens. But after nearly 2.59 million American soldiers fought in Vietnam—a great many of them out of a sense of duty—the communist, anti-colonialist government expelled the United States from what it considered its own ravaged country for trespassing.

My career apparently in ruins, I climbed into the bus—until then a vehicle of opportunity and adventure. Noting my reflection, I was surprised that a few raindrops streaking the window had moistened my cheeks.

Footnotes:
1. Alexander Canduci, *The Greatest Lies* in *History.* New York: Metro Books/ Murdoch Books Pty Limited, 2009, pp. 227-37.
2. *In So ward Abend und Morgen.* Verlag der Arche, Peter Schifferli, 1955.

10. Geodyssey IV: The Sewer of Despond

The inertia of the overland coach challenges our hands, arms, shoulders, torso, and legs as several of us guys lean against it. As we push, our boots churn a little faster, the resistance diminishes, the tailpipe coughs, and the vehicle chugs downhill by itself, then turns around. Its coating of Turkish snow-desert—as high as the clouds it merged with—is begrimed by Iranian dust.

Soon all the passengers crowded together and bounced away from the customs building where Tom and I had unrolled our sleeping bags near a painted line that separated a big room into two countries. Adventure continued with a daylong ride accompanied by exotic pop songs piped in over tinny speakers. "I admired this woman's fancy purse," said my companion, "till it moved its wing." Once the bus skidded to a halt as a camel crossed the road while bucking against its driver and kicking up dust with ornery, rangy legs.

That night in Tabriz we were hustled from our hotel into a cab or police car by two unidentified men whose words were volubly unintelligible. At a police station, we registered as itinerants. The next day we made the acquaintance of friendly young man who gave us a tour that included a carpet factory. There, children, smiling at the visitors, valued for their dexterous fingers, tied tot-knots—which fastened them to an 8' X 10' life. Our guide also introduced us to a missionary couple who had met at my college and who kindly let us stay with them. Learning that they associated beards with riffraff-drifters, I had mine shaved for the equivalent of eight cents.

In Teheran, we visited the parents of my schoolmates, also missionaries, whose cautiousness turned to an invitation after an evening of laughter. The city held underemployed, drably-clothed men, and it jumbled together the modern with the medieval, the racket of traffic with the rustle of the burka. I assumed that its citizens venerated the Shah because they displayed his photograph in many a store window.

Two rails ran five hundred miles eastward through darkness to Mashhad, a holy city, we were told. The travelers' grapevine warned us not to shove eastward through bandit-ridden

Afghanistan but to circumvent it. So we headed south on a bus that departed at 7 a.m. rather than the promised 5 a.m. Once Tom and I, along with a fellow from New Zealand, sang "Old MacDonald" and drew laughter with the *oink-oink*. But by then I had come down with sickness in muscle and bone, one adumbrated by a fierce headache on the train that had pulled night to day. Our seat-backs extended only to the neck, so over and over again I tried to lean against the jerking window with my head wrapped in a new Turkish scarf made of yellow-dyed wool. The glass was a seismograph that registered each vibration, tilt, and bump. Compulsively I would tear off a piece of chapati (round, unleavened bread made with whole wheat flour) and onto it squeeze sweetened condensed milk from a tube.

At one roadside place a man steadied me as I almost fell into a samovar. But at a smoky, low-ceilinged place furnished with benches and metal tables, I ate the tastiest food in the world—*chelo kebab*, a skewer of sausage-like pieces of lamb over a pile of steaming rice. At one stop I climbed a hill for a view of the December desert, lost my balance on the way down, and made a three-point landing on hands and yellow-flashing skull, injured by the very earth I had surveyed.

Then the bus broke down and for ten hours we sat while someone tried to get a new bearing or whatever. In desperation Tom and I spun a dream of Ceylon: we would loll on the beach, sip from a coconut, dally with maidens who wore fronds from the same tree, then purchase an old boat and sail across the Indian Ocean to the Malay Peninsula.

When the reconstituted coach pulled into Zahedan after fifty-one hours—an average of 12 miles an hour—this vision faded. Yet I was unable to fall asleep for the third day and walked about the town and our rented room like a zombie. We were too impatient to hang around for five days for the weekly passenger train eastward, so we decided to risk the daily water-train to Baluchistan and then try hitchhiking.

Our gloves serving as tickets, we grasped the ladder of a flat tank-car and climbed to its railed top, hauling our gear by strap and string. Our fellow passengers included the fellow from New Zealand, a grinning boy of about twelve years old who kept his hands and arms in a boxing pose, and a bearded elder who sat on the contents of a gunny sack next to his sheep. Everyone got along well. Tom and I were relieved to be moving again even though it would be only fifty miles into the desert, maybe thirty.

At the end of the jaunt in Nok Kundi, a woman with leathery hands tightened a blanket-like garment across her mouth and nose against the sandy dust, an element that further blurred the distinction between the small buildings and the terrain from which they'd been made. Her children scooped up a few pieces of coal from beside the locomotive. This was a border post town, so after taking a photo I found myself wrestling Tom's camera away from a soldier who shouted either "Neex" or "Feeneesh," all-purpose international negatives.

We positioned ourselves by a bend in the road near a primitive rest stop but finally couldn't stand to sit. So up went the packs and down the highway we walked, I in a half-trance. Closer and closer we moved toward a fort shaped from the gray-white-beige stone and the bare mountains surrounding it. I equated motion with survival. No vehicles appeared, so nobody could even roll past our upturned thumbs. I finally lay down on the cold pebbles with my coat as a buffer and my knapsack as a pillow. Thoughts were inseparable from aching head and arms, sickness, and fatigue. After a while I stumbled to my feet and tottered up the rise to a privy. There in a kind of ceremony I held up my new journal, with its stiff, blue covers, and dropped it into the Sewer of Despond.

Some time later, on the horizon back toward Nok Kundi—was that a cloud of dust? In front of it a speck slowly resolved itself into a vehicle, a large black sedan, which seemed to drive off the celluloid from an old movie. Its oversize tires came to a halt. Tom asked the occupants, evidently seasoned travelers, if they would carry me to the oasis a few hours ahead called Dalbandin. They somehow mined a place for me in the back seat by fastening one more bundle to a rack on the trunk or roof. Tom reached in, stuffed my knapsack on my lap, vowed to meet me there, and shut the door.

That night I continued to rest, delighted to see trees again with their bark, cells, and growth-rings. My benefactors and I shared a table at a very simple restaurant where my order for chicken curry produced a squawk that was equally loud and brief. Apprehensive about my rendezvous with Tom, I tottered back to a rented hovel, marveling at the stars as numerous as the grains of sand. They reminded me of time my father, driving all night, stopped at the California border for an agricultural inspection. We three boys woke up, climbed out of the Plymouth wagon, and slowly spun dumbfounded at our first view of the entire firmament.

Now I was wrapping myself in the bedroll when I sensed a little commotion near the hanging-flap-of-a-door. The sound of a growl went through my body like a shock as I remembered seeing a few dogs that hung around the place. Vulnerable and fragile, I grabbed my flashlight, exposed two pairs of reflections, and, galvanized by fright, yelled and clapped away the scavengers.

Chah-eee…. Chah-eee, the Pakistani vendors would drone on the platform, then through the raised window hand clay cups of tea mixed with sugar and water-buffalo milk. Tom and I, our reunion successful thanks to his ride in the VW bus of an Indian citizen, had caught this train in Quetta, just below Afghanistan. Our journey from Dalbandin had been measured by actual milestones that stuck out along the rugged highway. Now we rode in a modern railroad car bearing an insignia that to my gratification gave credit to the United States for funding. I seemed restored after a doctor at the oasis had handed me some powdered medicine, and we spent the day placidly gazing out the windows or lounging on the steps as green crops passed with a clatter. The noise made conversation difficult but we often talked inside, maybe with a Pakistani who knew some English.

Once as I watched from the step in a dreamy mood induced by the flow of the adjoining rails and fields, I realized that if a train should pass from the opposite direction, it could wreak havoc on my perch. Out of curiosity I slowly leaned forward and peered to the right—at a black rotundity a few cars up that yawed like the Phantom Boat of Doom. Before I could even gauge its speed, I whipped back, kept my eyes hard open, and clenched the handrail. *Just hold on.* The blast sucked my eardrums and churned the air, and after a few roaring blurry moments, the green crops reappeared, strangely composed, unlike me.

The sun woke us to cold air outside our bedrolls. "Randy, can you believe this?" Lifting my head from the pillow made of a shirt stuffed with clothing, I found my companion leaning on his elbow and pointing from the wooden rack to the floor and a tidy orange blaze. Several passengers hunkered down and rubbed their hands near its smoking scraps. In the row of seats next to the windows other travelers had spent the night sitting up; one man possessed only a shawl to buffer the cold, and I watched his fits of shivering with pity. He sniffed loudly and wiped his nose on his sleeve. I kept wanting to get down and lend him my coat, but I dared not risk catching a bug, so I kept my raiment and stayed uneasy to this day.

My knapsack was heavier by the weight of an oversized tubular key, an accidental souvenir of the hotel in Tabriz. My pocket contained half a molar that had broken off when I bit into a seedy confection on the platform at Quetta. Now some unknown food or drink was beginning to cause me an internal problem. Tom reminded me that I was carrying a well-traveled bottle of paregoric, and I now sipped it like a wino.

In Lahore, naughty of name, chaotic of streets, we spent the night on woven-rope cots that had escape-holes. Then onto another train we climbed and headed ninety miles north to Sialkot. There a man eventually arrived, showed us to a two-wheeled cart, wrapped himself in a blanket, and took the reins. He had been sent by my classmate's parents, Dr. and Mrs. Robert A. Foster. They operated the Christian Training Institute, which provided an education through tenth grade. As dusk fell, we faced backward, the horse slowly clip-clopped toward the city's outskirts, and bells on the harness reminded me of hometown wagon rides. Now and then a car overtook the pedestrians, cyclists, or other tongas. The air, damp and cool, carried the scent of horses, grass, food, and cooking smoke that muted the sunset. Overhead green branches decorated the road.

Ushered into their home, a former British courthouse, we observed a high-ceilinged hall, a warming wood-stove, and an alien familiar object: a tree with colored lights draping its needles.

11. Proprioception: "We Have Hefted the Plates"

And we declare with words of soberness, that an angel of God came down from heaven, and he brought and laid before our eyes...the plates and the engravings thereon.... [W]e have seen and hefted, and know of a surety that the said [Joseph Smith, Jr., the translator] has got the plates of which we have spoken.

Testimony of three witnesses, then eight, *The Book of Mormon* (1830).

Lifting an Akkadian fragment or a mangy dog, shoving a gearshift, trudging through snow or gauging its density between powder and slush, yanking a pod from a tree or lowering a bottle from a train, pushing a recalcitrant bus, shaping manure from a water buffalo into a fuel-pancake—all these actions require earthlings to monitor our balance, the positions of our torso-limbs-fingers, and the degree of opposition we encounter.

A gym-goer can make a machine return a certain degree of resistance by inserting a popper-pin in the stack of 10-pound plates. A weight-watcher can stand on the scale to quantify the body's opposition to gravity. But humans (as well as other vertebrates) must monitor the degree of resistance internally in order to perform any motor skill. A lucky batter, for example, feels the "sweet spot" where the ball meets the fullest opposition to the swing and thus rebounds with the most force.

Our network of self-monitoring is called proprioception—i.e., self-perception, awareness of internal signals rather than of external stimuli directly. Judged "underappreciated" by one authority **(1)**, it is usually taken for granted unless compromised by fatigue, drugs, injury, or disease.

As an example of this last cause, a touch of multiple sclerosis left a friend of the author's unable to direct his foot or sense its position. He reports:

> My walk-aid lifts my toe (so I do not stumble) and turns out my foot (so my base is wider) for stability. The walk-aid's computer times the assistance to coincide with the lifting of my leg as I begin a step.

According to R.A. Schmidt and C.A. Wrisberg, this system allows human beings to monitor "the positions of the joints, the forces produced in the muscles and the orientation of the body in space." The term overlaps with *kinesthesis*, the perception of movement during motor activity, and has become synonymous with it.**(2)** This internal system gives feedback about what S. Coren and L. Ward term "our continual battle against gravity," as well as the "tension, compression, or twisting forces on the muscles, tendons, or joints of limbs."(3) It relies on receptors in these areas, along with those in the skin and in layers of tissue beneath it that can detect pressure.

Proprioceptive skill varies with age and practice. Once I noticed some children frolicking on a porch that was low but un-railed, so I watched them out of the corner of my eye. A boy suddenly teetered on the edge as I lunged while reaching out my palm, cupped it under his falling hair, and let his head become heavier as I slowed it to a stop just above the brick walk.

How does this internal GPS work? Specialized nerves relay information to the cortex and cerebellum by way of the spinal cord. *Muscle spindles* make up one set. These narrow tubes with tapered ends, imbedded in the fibers of a muscle, register its changing length. Another set, the *Golgi tendon organs*, detect the forces produced in a muscle when it contracts. As for balance, it is monitored by receptors in the *vestibular apparatus* (inner ear).(4)

Proprioception often cooperates with the sense of touch—i.e., the skin's ability to monitor surfaces. But signals of texture reach the brain from cutaneous nerves rather than from underlying ones. To clarify the distinction, here are a few imagined testimonials from the story of Rapunzel, chapter to come:

Husband: "As the petals of the rampion brushed my skin, I pulled its leaves until they broke with the sound of finger-snapping Fate."

Wife: "I ran the leaves around my mouth with my tongue, then chomped them, green tooth-grist."

Narrator: "Wrapped in a soft blanket, the newborn weighed as much as two hearts."

Sorceress: "With the needle under my thumb, I pushed and pulled it through the tightly encircled cloth."

Prince: "To my royal fingers the filaments streaming down from her head were sun-rays, yet they held me fast as curiosity overcame gravity."

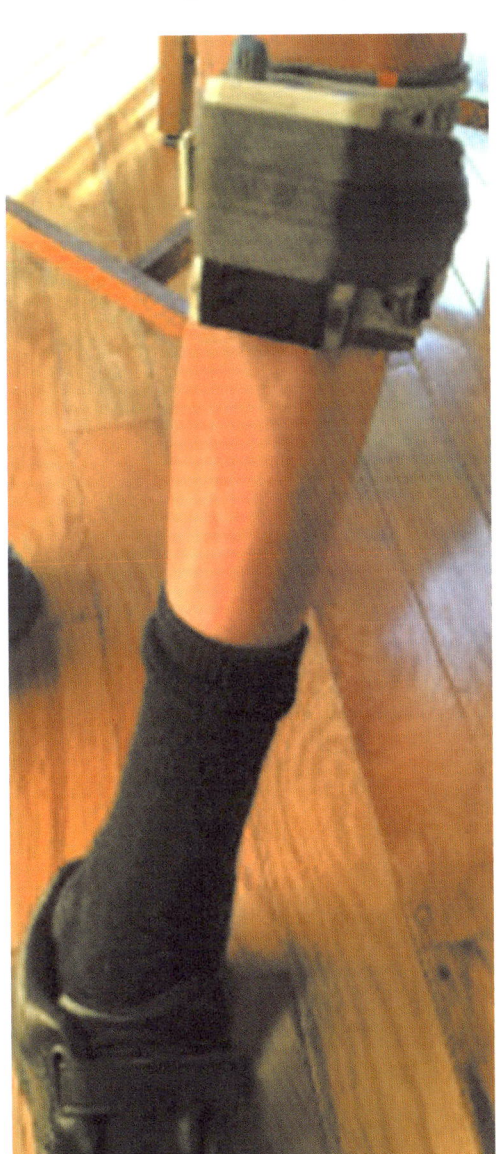

Courtesy Robert W. Matthews.

Sorceress: "The threads of the girl's treachery pressed like wires against my cheek, and as I squeezed the scissor-blades, joints rejoiced."

As in these examples, proprioception very often works along with the eyes. "Look, feel it!" says Marge as she hands me a pail of blueberries. Sometimes (to use a baseball analogy) right-fielder Proprioception traps the ball missed by shortstop Sight. For instance the apparently empty carton dips under one unseen egg; the about-to-be-crumpled bag signals a mystery weight (luckily a miniature Kit Kat); a runty loaf of wheat bread surprises the hand and arm with its denseness; a heavy glass beer mug almost reaches the forehead before Golgi-and-spindle correct for its lightweight plastic.

We might hoist a teapot to estimate its water level. But even experts can misjudge, as when a pair of mail clerks took turns weighing an envelope by hand: "Three," said one, "Four" declared the other, "Two ounces" decreed the scale. One comedian, Jack Benny, demonstrated a talent for weight-discrimination during his TV show. His pants were hanging on a rack, and after his valet took a coin out of the pocket to tip a deliveryman, Jack returned, lifted his trousers, and asked who'd taken out the quarter.**(5)**

Not only the eyes but the ears can complement this system. Little Katie determined whether or not a box still contained its audiotape partly by shaking and holding it to her ear.

Proprioception can fail us. One day in fourth grade Tommy Hollinger presented a gift to the teacher, a sort of bouquet with six red roses. Manufactured at his dad's "Shop," it was preserved in water and enclosed in a glass globe about eight inches in diameter. Not to be countenanced. Was it not a version of the polished apple? Certainly a reminder that the only object I associated with my father's job was a slide rule. Worst of all, its petals saturated with color and its ever-unfaded, ever-undrowned flowers—magic! What I'd now call a virtual reliquary. So when the teacher stepped out, up went its square base to the top of my head, the crown I deserved. Balancing it, I pranced around before my alarmed and giggling schoolmates. A sudden absence of weight felt by neck and torso smashed with unsought liberation, and we all gazed open-mouthed at the pool of stem-petal-shards.

The traditional paradigm of the Five Senses ignores proprioception. Yet that worn-out doctrine will probably be handed down to children like the story of George Washington and the cherry tree—an apocryphal chop that would have required signals from muscles, tendons, joints, and tissues as to shape, weight, position, angle, force, and speed.**(6)**

Forty years after becoming deposed as King of the Classroom, I introduced my daughter's elementary school peers to the physical sense of position and resistance. First they described an apple in writing: not only its shape, colors, smell, taste, and sound when chomped, but its opposition when squeezed, bitten, or lifted. Before the next day's session they performed some kind of physical activity or skill and then recorded any proprioceptive challenges it entailed. One student wrote with an enthusiasm that outran orthography:

> We played Mircey [Mercy], pushing, pulling, gravity, played hand game, and turned around pulling each others arms in a circle, arm wrestling, hand holding, lifting leg with great force, lifting up me. When we where playing hand games, we forced our hands to- gether, jumping.

Another child reported that while sketching with a pencil, you have to bear down harder in some places to make them darker. Another fellow warned about applying too much pressure when cutting wood with a "bansaw": you push, pull, or twist slowly so the blade won't break and cut off your fingers. Another student applied makeup to Jennifer—squeezing the sponge to apply the foundation, even pulling her face just enough to lighten the eye-shadow. Allison made cookies:

"I felt resistance when I stirred with the mixer. I had to keep it in the bowl. When I cracked the eggs I had to be carefull to get it in the bowl. I had to reach for the bowl. The eggs were light, but I couldn't hit them very hard or they would break everywhere.(7)"

Children who become more conscious of this faculty will better appreciate their earthly involvement. As a bonus they will empathize with Uncle Wiggly Longears and his mouse friend as they labor to roll their cheese-wheel out of a ditch and back up the hill.(8) It was the sense of our own babies' weight that evoked my curiosity about what my colleague explained was proprioception. As the years passed they, too, would notice these signals. Andrea on her Halloween loot: "Want to see how heavy my bag is?" Katie on an envelope that held Girl Scout cookie-profits: "Gol, feel how heavy this money thing is!"

Even imaginary characters have this ability. Robinson Crusoe made his way into the body of the shipwreck, where he "felt several casks, and loosened them with the crow[bar], but could not break them up." He also felt "a roll of English lead, and could stir it, but it was too heavy to remove" (1719). Can an imaginary character sense proprioception figuratively? From a novel by Richard O. Collin: "The Adviser's body is leaden because his personal biological clock is still synchronized with Greenwich and the Prime Meridian. In England, it is still the middle of the night."(9)

A communion wafer draws on a sensory armamentarium. Eyes report its round, white thinness; tongue reports its smooth texture and helps the nose register its bland taste; ears note the ritual crack as the officiant breaks it; skin reports its smoothness. But other specialized nerves appreciate its essential, quasi-mystical quality: near-weightlessness, which hovers between the earthly and the ethereal, true angel food, holy Necco.

Consider the spud. To lift it a cook must sense how much effort the fingers, hand, and arm must expend. To peel it, one hand must do the turning while the other shoves a blade against the skin at just the right speed and angle; to test it for doneness, fingers pinch it;

teeth chew it by sending feedback to the periodontal ligament as to how much force must be exerted.

The faint residual ability to grind this vegetable saved one dying person. In February, 1945, Ernest Lion had spent days riding an open coal car while forced to travel from Auschwitz on his second journey to Buchenwald:

> Once I passed out from hunger and clearly felt myself falling into a deep sleep, more severe than I have ever experienced since. I remember vividly how I slipped peacefully and without pain into a coma…. Then someone stuck a raw potato into my mouth. I chewed some of it and its juices slowly revived me. It took a long time to regain total consciousness.**(10)**

Not long before this event, Alzbeta was forced to use her own remaining strength to coordinate palms, muscles, tendons, and joints as a foxhole-and grave-digger for Germans. (How much Lebensraum does a man need?)

The life of each person includes kinesthetic highlights, positive and negative. A dozen of my own offer a precedent for yours:

> The old-fashioned, reel-type lawn mower, a Briggs & Stratton, apportioned half its weight to me and half to my mother, who had driven across town so I wouldn't have to push the machine home. I felt a twinge of guilt as her hands and wrists strained to lift it by handle and wheel into the back of the station wagon.
>
> Marching along the entire parade route, I held the American flag at an Iwo Jima angle as my torso and legs supported the bottom of the pole, which sank into a pouch attached to a wide belt.
>
> Scaffold, ladder, and bicycle: a combination not to be missed. So with one arm and shoulder, I found the balancing point of the wheeled frame and with the free hand grasped the rungs. Soon I was riding up and down the planks alongside a new church until a policeman escorted me home to my father (who shook his head as if unable to understand).

Four arms and four sprinting legs shared the weight of a horizontal extension-ladder as it bounced. When my father and I reached the smoke-filled house, we hoisted the rungs hand-over-hand until they were nearly vertical, then tilted them onto the roof of the front porch.

As I carried the shiny brass cross at the head of a robed procession, it was surprisingly heavy—"Almost like a weapon," I thought.

For the tall grandfather's clock we would provide a kind of battery by pulling one of the two sash-weights down with a cranking noise. At bedtime we would gently restrain the edge of the pendulum to prevent its strikes on the quarter hours and hour—at midnight a gong-smasher.

As Tom and I explore Halifax after rough seas, why do the sidewalks seem to roll, the bridges to rock, and the stairs to rise up and down, making us almost landsick?

To don a heavy pack:
- Set it on floor, straps toward you.
- Bend over and grasp top of left strap with right hand. Keeping knees bent, lean on right leg, lift pack, keeping right arm bent and close to torso.
- Straighten up quickly while twisting to the right and raising right elbow slightly to help hoist backpack.
- Hunch the pack slightly into the air with your torso and swing half-circle onto the right side of your back so that the left strap flips toward your left shoulder-blade.
- At same time, reach with the left hand, hunching the pack slightly off your back to make a space for the left hand to grab it.
- Force left hand under strap, pull it up left shoulder and over left arm.
- Begin to adjust straps for evenness, stand up, and adjust the straps for symmetry and the pack for weight.

On the platform of the Illinois Central Railroad, I grasped the handle of a woman's suitcase and found myself tugging an anvil—"It's full of books, my daughter's"—which I hauled the length of the train. (I did get a ride to the dormitory, but also a later one by ambulance when I could not stand up.) More of the proprio-positive examples:

As I carried our firstborn, bobbing and patting her, she screeched *Colic!* with wide-open gums. When at last she fell asleep against my shoulder, I treasured the weight of her head and body, indignant that such a burden could be measured by the pound.

In France, dare we cross the bridge against an invisible current far above the River Gard? I judged the risk an acceptable trade-off for adventure and invited both daughters to go along. Holding hands at times, we leaned against the Mistral, proceeding in irregular tacks along the ancient aqueduct, skirting the rectangles that opened to the level below, testing our grip and balance at every step, sometimes crawling. On the other side we stood up and proudly waved at Mom.

Kicking for lap after lap, down the pool and up, I would raise one arm out of the water, cock it behind my head, and plunge my hand down and backward in line with my shoulders, rather than close to my waist—in the path of most resistance and thus of speed—as I would raise the other hand into the air. Finally I pulled myself up the steps with dripping arms and legs, maintained my balance across the wet tiles, and penciled an X in a square to mark my two-hundredth half-mile.

The sense of resistance is often expressed figuratively. Some words only hint at the original metaphors, such as the nouns *poise* and *gravitas,* while many phrases still retain a faded image:

> Put your shoulder to the wheel, stand on the shoulders of those before, shrug it off, get government off our backs, take a load off; elbow your way in; leave someone hanging or twisting in the wind; reach out to, lean on, fall for, strong-arm, shake off, yank around, or bend over backwards for someone; drop the ball or get it rolling; dig in your heels, twist the knife; roll with the punches, pull your punches, pull your weight, have pull, pull someone's chain, push someone's button, when push comes to shove; don't mean to pry; weigh an idea, toss it out, catch it, or kick it around; touch bases; get wound up or wind down; bite the bullet; be light-headed, light-fingered, light-hearted, heavy-hearted, lead-footed; words worth their weight in gold.

In John Bunyan's allegory, Christian learns that his city will be burned by heavenly fire, so he fears that he will be undone by "a burden that lieth hard upon me" (i.e., his iniquities, Psalms 38:4). "What shall I do to be saved?" he asks frantically. Warned by the Evangelist to fly the oncoming judgment of the world, he runs away in search of eternal life.

His bundle almost sinks him into the Slough of Despond (as the weight of his sins makes him despair). He learns, however, that he should be content to bear it until he comes to a place of deliverance. He struggles up a hill to a cross, where his burden is loosed from his shoulders, falls off his back, and tumbles into a sepulcher, causing him to feel "glad and lightsome." (The sins of the long-struggling Christian have been forgiven by the sacrificial death of Jesus.) After crossing the river of death, he finally reaches Mount Zion, the heavenly Jerusalem, a shining city of winged harpers and gold-paved streets. So Bunyan enlists what else but proprioception, the most earth-bonding of senses, to help believers make their way safely through this world to the next.

Footnotes:
1. Joan Piroch, Professor of Psychology, Coastal Carolina University. Personal communication.

2. *Motor Learning and Performance*, 2nd ed. Champaign, Illinois: Human Kinetics, 2000, p. 91.
3. *Sensation and Perception*, 3rd ed. San Diego: Harcourt, 1984, p. 259.
4. K.G. Pearson, "Proprioceptive Sensory Feedback." *Encyclopedia of Life Sciences* Vol.15, pp. 263-64. See also R. Wells, "'The Jar Went Heavy in my Hand': How the Written Word Captures Proprioception." *Bridges Online Journal*, Winter 2008, Coastal Carolina University.
5. George Burns, with David Fisher. *All My Best Friends*. New York: Putnam, 1989, p. 279.
6. One example is the charming *I Like to See: A Book About the Five Senses*, by Jean Tymms, illustrated by June Goldsborough (Racine, WI: Whitman, 1973). The examples of Touch—sand, ice cubes, pebbles, rose petals, kittens, and pillows—certainly illustrate textures. But along with this touching comes stimulation of the tissues, muscles, and joints of the hand. They register both position and resistance while sculpting grains into a turret, lifting a pebble or ice cube and exploring its shape, and noting the near-weightlessness of the petal. The fingers, hands and arms register the shifting weight of the kitten, and the neck senses the easy receptivity of the pillow.
7. Michelle L. Schroder (Mercy) and Allison Canady Daly (cookies). By permission, 2011.
8. Howard R. Garis, *Uncle Wiggly's Picture Book*. Illustrated by Lansing Campbell. New York: Platt & Munk, 1922, 1924, 1940, pp. 116-17.
9. *The Man with Many Names*. New York: St. Martin's, 1995, pp. 26-27
10. *The Fountain at the Crossroad,* p. 38.

12: The Estate III: "Stoney Reality"

The meadow of dream has little to do with stoney reality and its harrows and reapers. May Days © The University of Iowa Press, 1988, p. 3. Used with permission.

So declares Samuel F. Pickering, Jr., in a volume given to me by a neighbor, Margie Keith, owner of a used-book store. As for my own dream, it pertained to stones.

And it began with Jane Cundiff's exhortation. She wrote that people should mow less grass, and instead plant clover and wildflowers to help feed bees and butterflies, insects that seem threatened on several fronts. Half a year earlier I had saved a lone honeybee (*Apis mellifera*) in Paris by plucking its scrambling *cul* out of an espresso cup with a spoon, so why not make a wholesale rescue?

The Wellses agreed to an environmental compromise. Marge would plant wildflowers in a rocky hillside of weeds, blackberry bushes, and volunteer trees. Across our section of Annie Lane to the west I would plant clover after removing rocks in bare clay spots that spread erratically over a semi-grassy field. (As a tangential benefit, why not a lawn-souvenir of the suburb?)

Our acquaintance—of accent Brooklyn, Buddhist of outlook—had scraped the area flat with tractor and blade. Yet only partly level because it slopes to both north and west. In local fashion Bill accepted a small amount of money and a truckload of barter—hemlock planks from our temporarily dismantled deck, future siding for a shed. Afterward we had planted the area in grass—a "monoculture" to Jane—in order to make a rough yard for grandchildren that would also accentuate the clearing between house and forest.

Rocks first. Everyone who plants in this area must deal with the Rocky Mountains of the East. Once icy and heaven-threatening, they had cashed in over the eons and left small change scattered all around, coins big and small, drab and colorful. Obstructions to blades, seeds, and roots, these fragments had fed rock-crushers during the construction of the Blue Ridge Parkway. As Jean Thomas Schaeffer remembers, "My grandma was paid a total of $100 for fifty dump-truck loads of rocks—all from her cornfield, just after harvest. She said it was the only time she ever 'got something for nothing.'"**(1)**

Bill's scraper had shoved thousands of our rocks into miniature lateral moraines. Over the next couple of years, I had plucked and hauled the largest ones from the field to one side of the driveway as a marker and barrier for vehicles negotiating snow. I had hired a couple of young guys to work for several hours, unbeknownst to them a former young guy myself.

Author vs. reality.

My tools were a (1) a level-head rake with twelve sturdy tines, (2) a spade, (3) a flexible rubber tub, and (4) a faded red wheelbarrow. Kneeling in my dirt-stained work-pants, as if to Gaia herself, I would rotate the head of the rake to the left and jab its left corner into the clay. My right hand would grasp the handle toward the front and from underneath, while my left, toward the tapered back, would grasp it from above. To protect my generous scalp from cold, wind, or sun, I wore the cloth hat—broad-rimmed, chin-strapped—given to me by Tom when I lost mine and risked the Florida sun. To protect my knees I wore long trousers with knee-patches of brown dirt. I also sported yellow-orange leather gloves with reinforced palms, frequently taking off the right one so as to pluck stones more easily.

Besides the sense of touch, no fewer than three others helped me do the job.

Hearing allowed me to perceive a scrape or clink that meant "fragment." Several times it also registered the duller sound of a root left when the area had been clear-cut and bulldozed. My ears also confirmed that a tossed stone had plunked into the tub, banged into the wheelbarrow, or silently disappeared into the grass.

As for sight, I easily noticed many pebbles and rocks lying on the surface. These I would rake or pluck up. Others angled partway out, and others revealed themselves only while being pried from hacked clay. Sometimes the tilling process required me to distinguish between a clod that pretended to be a rock and vice versa, no doubt morphodite. I could tell a rock by its edges and sometimes by its color—not the earthy brown but white or gray. A few times I was surprised to spot one of these inorganic shapes lying in the grass as if trusting in shaded immobility. My prospecting eyes would find small areas where moss hinted at a potential non-rolling stone that took up space for soil and water. Once or twice I turned up a cherry pit, and two or three times a black rock that resolved into a hickory shell, evidence of the clear-cut forest.

Collaborating with sight and hearing was proprioception. I maintained balance, fittingly, with rocks—tiny crystals called otoliths. They rolled around my inner ear as I tried to stay upright on knees or feet, to lean forward, or to twist. And I accomplished other exertion (along with an assist to balance) via specialized cells that sent telegrams to my brain. *Poke harder. Quit jabbing & prying. Probe around edge. Give up, stand up. Pick up shovel.* They would also wire the degree of force needed by arms and legs to lift a trophy to the barrow. They also helped me calibrate the amount of wrist-flick needed to toss rocks of various weights into the tub. And when this vessel became too gravity-grudging as I slid it along: *Lift handle. Dump into barrow.*

This interaction of body with earth helped me feel physically whole even as I continued to carry off the detritus of a mountain.

If I had to rise to grab the shovel, I first lay the end of the rake-handle on the ground to point at the invisible rock to be pried up. A couple of times the spade clinked short as I probed around a hidden rock that grew larger and larger to a slab; reluctantly I abandoned hopes of extraction. I had to remind myself that the bees wouldn't care about a tiny patch of missing clover. "It can serve as home plate." Another time I had to poke-and-shovel deeply around an iceberg-like remnant that, luckily, had broken in half underground so it could reach the rock garden in two one-wheeled trips. Sometimes a find crumbled as I worked it, potential slurry that would make its way down to the stream that crossed at the bottom of Annie Lane and drowned in Dodd Creek. Sometimes the tell-tale clink reminded me of clamming, or of paddling as I stretched the long handle this way and that, sometimes changing arms.

When the wheelbarrow got full enough—of pebbles, gravel-sized rocks, and palm-dippers—I leaned and pushed till it reached the crest of our narrowing ridge. There I tried to manage its roll down the steep side onto a former logging-trail. After tipping the load into one of its declivities, I pushed the barrow back up the side of the hill via one zigzag and one rest. Halting near the top, I caught my breath and bent over long enough for blood pressure to override medicine. After two such hauls and about two hours, Bees' Best Friend thought it wise to quit. In the carport I pulled the gloves onto the handles of the wheelbarrow, their fingers sticking out backwards to welcome the pusher like a whimsical installation.

In the field again, this time with white swellings on my right palm that recalled my first job. Would "Grandma" Allen want me to sweep her sidewalk? So down the long series of panels on Cottage Ave. I waved the broom. Should I also straw-whip the indentations between panels? Five feet after five feet, I at last met the other slabs at the corner with Newton. But before turning south, what was this little white rise on my palm? After another half-hour, and further rising, they grasped a twenty-five cent piece.

Now I tried to focus on ambient sounds. My inspiration was a book that Andrea had given me as a retirement present: *How Now: 100 ways to celebrate the present moment*. One way was to let each sound register separately.**(2)** I did notice a rooster's mindless *crogito ergo sum*, but the tweets and chirps, the breeze swooshing through the grove of white pines planted as a windbreak, the occasional faraway moo, and the hum of traffic on Rt. 221 distracted me from telltale clicks of steel against rock.

Each day, windy or hot, cold or warm (or both), the earth moist or baked, the weather sunny or sprinkling, I would force myself to quit, remembering that earlier sessions had knocked me out. I tried for a one-hour limit, but then I looked around—"If I can just get that one brown spot with its random stones…." When I did slowly rise to my feet, I beheld clay tentacles everywhere. "If I can just get to that bareness around the maple tree…." I noticed that the surface looked grassy from the side, but from atop it, inexcusably ill-maintained. Abandoning lawn, I settled for yard.

No Southern Appalachian gems such as garnet, amazonite, amethyst, or unakite. No local soapstone, which had already turned to suds. Certainly no fairy stones—staurolyte crystals forged by heat and pressure as the earth's crust squeezed up the Appalachians. No chance of turning up an ancient Roman game-piece carved from marble, like the one Jane and Ken spotted in a newly-tilled Tunisian field of Carthage and gave me as a birthday present.**(3)** And only faux arrowheads were revealed as the sun inclined at different angles.

A rainfall exposed previously hidden stones. Did my blister itself not resemble a fragment of quartz? One day the expanse of unplucked 57 in the driveway gave me a start. Another time I just *had* to pick up one more rock as I rolled gear toward carport, so I stuck it in my pocket. I remembered one of the people I'd interviewed in an oral history project. Working for a cannery in the autumn, he had seined for mullet and stacked pile-shares of them on the beach: "Don't put one in your pocket!"

To pass time, I recalled stones in my life. Again I watched my father toss a flat one sidearm into a lake and cause it to reappear—even two or three times. I remembered the stone that, as a boy, I had hurled from our backyard toward the street to harass an interloper. "Hey, Curly!" Mean-spirited turf-guarding—was this a stage to be worked through before I could resist the cry of the tribe? *Clink.* Irish neighborhood vs. Polish.... On and on. *Plunk.* Maybe there's a feud in Japan between Sumo and Sushi. *Pluck.*

Rocks paradoxical: as ballast they had anchored many a rail for rollin' Randall & Tom. Rocks personal: in rural Asia I learned that a stone in the field was Charmin. Rocks geomagical: I recalled scrambling up a great cone of boulder fragments in France, Mt. Mezenc, from under which a torrent wrenched northward as the Loire.

Rarely did I have any consequential thoughts. Was I was becoming the primitive "Man with a Rake?" I did remember that "scruple" originally meant a stone caught in a sandal. And a few rock-walled churches drifted onto The Estate, at least in thought; they had been constructed in the area's social and geographic wilds by a Presbyterian Prometheus, Bob Childress (b. 1890).**(4)** The practice of lapidation did cross my mind—community supported execution—and I remembered a frightening story by Shirley Jackson called "The Lottery." And I thought of the student from Viet Nam who was forced by the new regime to help dig a canal with her bare hands.

Most of my brainwaves, however, were trashy or techy. *Keep the green tub on your right, so you won't have to look for it. Good, keep your work area out of the shadow of the wheelbarrow.* I started to admire my rake, a Vigoro, and as always felt grateful to my homely and perennial Timberlands, lubricated only twice with neatsfoot oil. I regretted that I had ever down-talked our $39 wheelbarrow, even though it required an adjustment to the front bracket after each dump.

After every workout, I hung a long-sleeved shirt next to pants in the tool-room, their knees further stained umber and flaked with dirt. With blotches as badges, they recalled my dusty catcher's uniform. "Disgusting," said Marge. A couple of times I stretched a raincoat out to dry.

I did witness a single bee—bumble-rather than honey-. It circled a patch of established clover. O welcome omen! Getting to my feet, I admired its unpredictable winding course and its way of shaving the air with a tiny electric razor.

Encountering Jane in town, I asked her to kiss my blister and she did.

Now I had to get outside every day or I felt sluggish, and I asked Marge to call me "Rocky." Although my lower back hurt, it kept serving and strengthening—thanks to surgery a couple of decades earlier to snip the disk herniated when I carried that Samsonite Library. But the arch of one foot hurt, and my left shoulder had a twinge from rotating rake-tines and probing with them. Fred, a physical therapist, diagnosed it as a "crepitus" with an accuracy unalloyed by diplomacy. At my wife's encouragement, I took a day off.

Back at my lone work. Surprising dedication for a person who scorned the mechanical notion of a "purpose-driven life." "Randall," I thought, "You don't have to be Rumpelstiltskin and do the job overnight." *Plunk.* "And you're not Ivan Denisovich with his gulag rocks." *Clack.* Yet despite this compulsiveness streak, I enjoyed working with figurative harrows and reapers instead of metals and pedals in the gym.

Another pleasure: not tangling with the fire ant (*Solenopsis*) of South Carolina. I did turn up the many-legged crescent of a grub, and once a scrawny worm wriggled over the clay—a hardscrabble pioneer, good luck. And what's this? The tines disturbed wings, and I stopped to let the moth extricate itself from the scruff at the base of grass and weeds. Unsteadily it scrambled up a blade of grass, where it perched and regarded me with close-set black eye-dots. Its motion seemed a blessing after countless inert objects.

> I beseech you [it wanted to say], do me no harm. Am I not as pretty as I am delicate? These magical wings of starched silk [out they stretched]— I'm told that one waft can change the world. And these filaments above and below— eight of them, threads from the same air-catching fabric. [Dipping its left antenna ceremoniously:] You will find nothing more ethereal in this plot of land, which you will agree is rather uncultivated. *S'il vous plaît, laissez moi tranquille.* Dangerously exposed on this verdancy, I risk being appreciated by a mere stomach.

One day I hauled four sacks of compost in the Subaru with the intention of covering areas that were especially torn up by missing rocks. Bought at Slaughters' Nursery, the stuff had been aerated after growing-trays of mushrooms had been emptied. So the clover would receive a welcome of wheat straw, dolomite, fibrous peat, gypsum, crushed feathers, cottonseed meal, and peanut meal. All this would add flavor notes to the ultimate honey.

Another day I managed to stand up, looked around, and pronounced myself finished. The dumping-path below had become somewhat level, the half-acre revealed only an occasional rock to the untrained observer, and my palm has a constellation of calluses above the heart-line.

Now I scanned the heavens like any farmer. One auspiciously gray morning I pushed the rolling fountain of a spreader over the largest composted spots, then hand-sowed many others with the tiny pellets. After only minimal rain fell, I had to attach a line of hoses to the cistern and empty its modest collection of roof-water upon the crop. Now my job was to wait.

Mineral, vegetable, animal.

Footnotes:

1. *Raised on Songs and Stories: A Memoir of Place in the Blue Ridge.* Floyd, VA: Harvestwood Press, 2014, p. 81.
2. By Raphael Cushnir. San Francisco: Chronicle, 2005, p. 100.
3. For a vivid account of the Cundiffs' travels, see Jane's *Cobras, Kids & Pyramids: Adventures of a Teaching Couple in Pakistan, Bangladesh and Egypt.* Floyd, VA: New Haven Press, 2015. The author's outlook is sharp-eyed, broad-minded, appreciative, adventuresome, cheerful, philosophical, critical, and touched by mystical Sufism.
4. Richard S. Davids, *The Man Who Moved a Mountain,* Philadelphia: Fortress Press, 1970.

13. Geodyssey V: Longitude 88 E

No justice was dispensed in this rambling former courthouse but instead, health. The whack of its gavel dismissed my physical and emotional ailments.

The Fosters were not only good Christians but Good Sports. They had recently hosted the former president of Maryville College, Dr. Ralph Waldo Lloyd, and his wife. (The previous spring I had witness his symbolic retirement when he walked offstage during this verse of a hymn: "Time, like an ever-rolling stream/Bears all its sons away….") And now who should arrive but one stranger with a beard and one with amoeba. The courthouse was already a temporary home for one missionary on R & R, as well as for a couple from England; he'd come to help with the accounting, and she kindly sewed up the armpit of my coat. Both Mrs. Brazil and Mrs. Foster had a Mom-ness that did not go unappreciated.

Our hosts were often at work somewhere else. Dr. Foster spent most of the time at the Christian Training Institute, which may have educated Untouchables. Mrs. Foster (Aurel) would cheerfully drive off on official errands, although she was home long enough to break up a loud squabble between the cook and another member of the household staff. She showed me a series of placards she used to teach reading; each displayed a picture and its corresponding Urdu or Punjabi word: Fire, **Ag**; book, **Katab**…. One of the thoughtful things she did for me, her daughter's classmate, was to set up a reel-to-reel recorder that played a tape of Dvorak's *New World Symphony*. At times the name seemed ironic because America had become the Old World of No Return.

An American doctor, head of the Christian Hospital in Sialkot, gave me some medicine—as did the company of his lovely young daughter. When our hosts invited the area's missionaries for Christmas dinner, I suggested that we play musical chairs, and the result was comical near-chaos, the heartiest laughter coming from a rather severe lady in a fox-boa coat.

Tom recorded memories of his own a half-century later:

> I remember trying to call the Fosters when we arrived and that it took from a little after 9 in the morning until 4:30 p.m to get through. It turned out this was their first phone call in 38 years, so it must have involved a great deal of commotion. In Sialkot I stayed with a Muslim family, although Dr. Foster insisted I later give the Christians equal time, which I did. One memory is of having breakfast in the Muslim house and eating a curry so strong that

tears came to my eyes. On inquiring, it seemed as though poor people eat only two meals a day, so if breakfast is very spicy, they remember that they have in fact eaten.

On arriving, I remember looking through a perforated screen separating the cooking area from the living area. Beyond the screen were girls and a lot of giggling and smiles. My host invited them in and introduced me as a "cousin"; since I was part of the family, they were allowed to visit and talk with us. This made living there much more comfortable and the evening more casual. At night they would bring the water buffalo into the house to keep it safe and to provide body heat to the rest of us.

I also remember walking down a road once and seeing a young girl, maybe nine or ten, who would pick up the droppings of the buffalo and make patties to fit into her basket. This seemed strange to me, and when I passed close to her she looked up and said "Good morning" as clear as day. I about fainted. People told me that American cows were not so valuable as they only gave milk or meat. The water buffalo was much better because it made fuel (manure) and gave heat to the house at night. It also did work like running the cane mills, provided transportation when hooked to a cart, and furnished milk and meat at the end of its usefulness. It was a complete use of what the poor beast had to give.

Near the end of Cousin Tom's sojourns, I felt well enough to travel alone on a side trip to India. First I made my way back to Lahore with its motorbikes and sidewalk scribes, then rode a train across the border to Amritsar—still a rickety trestle over the crevasse of Partition. There, a rich pall of smoke-food-sewage hung at dusk over the streets. A second train (direction uncertain) carried me to Dehra Dun in the foothills of the Himalayas. As the taxi hair-pinned up to a former British hill station, the other passengers looked at the ground and exclaimed "Snow!" while I looked at the trees and thought "Monkeys!"

I hiked up the long, steep path through Mussouri, encountering a man whose huffing servants carried him in a sedan chair, and reached the Christian boarding school headed by the father of my classmates. No students around because winter meant vacation, while school in summer furnished a refuge from the heat. During my cordial stay, I learned that the school had "all of the luxuries and none of the necessities"—e.g., tinfoil. Boarding the overnight train, I had the entire compartment to myself. Its windows barred against thieves, its door locked by the Maharaja, its thick black-leather cushion spread with a bedroll as if by a servant, it began to click against rail-joints, a vibration to ears and body that reminded me of pedaling a tricycle between sidewalk panels. I awoke the next morning in Amritsar.

Back to the Fosters' after an uneventful but demanding journey: crowds with their indecipherable syllables, traffic with its buses, motorbikes and honking fumes, the slight pressure of looking un-brown.

In the courthouse, a mongoose hid in a closet; outside, trees bore green-and-yellow parrots, and the Himalayas of Jammu-Kashmir loomed rosy-cream on the horizon. A former Shangri La, it was now a violently contested area that I was warned not to visit.

I pedaled far out in the country, through the bright coolness, to stay overnight with Tom—a sojourn undertaken despite my uneasiness with poverty, sickness, and ignorance.

"I think you should understand the old machine," he declared, perhaps with more wisdom than I could summon, "before you build a new one." But some things were too easy to comprehend. According to the physician, Dr. Hamm, kids ran around barefoot in the dung and didn't make enough hydrochloric acid to kill the hookworm eggs that enter through the mouth. Women had young children and wrinkles. I was touched, however, by Mrs. Foster's regret that change would destroy many wonderful old customs. One that we both no doubt disliked, on the other hand, was purdah, the seclusion of women from the public eye. Already constrained by their standard of living, they lived under house arrest, wrapped in a black shroud.

One morning we visited Master Preem's school, a classroom-playground. After songs, one group of kids sat reading aloud among themselves. Another sat with their washable writing tablets and bamboo pens while copying words that a young girl read aloud from a book. Another group did calisthenics while yelling in unison. While clouds of smoke from a nearby cooking-fire sometimes enveloped the schoolyard, villagers stood on roofs or poked their heads over the wall to observe the two "sahibs." The kids loved to stand by our chairs and read Urdu to us. (The author holds court in the photo.)

Everywhere we went some guy yelled "Tom!" and came over to shake hands. His prestige in the village of Buttar was damaged, however, when we tried to fit him, me, and my sleeping bag on one bicycle ride into Sialkot. After several entertaining false starts, I got our contraption rolling along the narrow, raised path between two fields. But toward us materialized a pile of sugar cane under two legs. I rang and rang the handlebar-bell to no avail, so off into the field we veered, and as we were picking ourselves up, a villager lent Tom his bike.

I undertook another solo jaunt, this one inside West Pakistan. By now I was making my way around with a bit of nerve, directions in hand, prodding the schematic to overcome the chaotic.

First I returned to Lahore, where a Filipino dentist, who had a contract with the missionaries, labored to build up the stump of tooth #15 with determination that overcame inadequate equipment.

Two days later my coal-smoking locomotive echoed between cuts as it chugged uphill toward what people spoke of as wild tribal areas. I got off in Taxila, where another classmate's father, an ophthalmologist, would annually remove cataracts from hundreds of folks who arrived in long lines, some with a crutch under one arm and a youngster on the other. While standing on a bluff as well as the ruins of an ancient town, I was surveying the vast plains below when I heard an inexplicable din. The air darkened as I perceived a mass of black specks that grew larger and took the shape of winged insects that now whirred past without cease, grasshoppers or locusts invading from the time of Alexander the Great.

In early January Tom and I bade affectionate farewell to our various hosts. I turned in my rented bicycle while he mailed a hookah to the U.S.A. After sitting in a roundabout for ten minutes, I was surrounded by two dozen people. A few were practicing their English on me when the owner of the shop jostled through the crowd and asserted that, although he had just spent time fixing the tire, the cycle belonged to another business. As we argued, the crowd swelled to forty-two. En masse we crossed the street, where he pointed out that the dealer was closed. I suggested that when the place opened, he could transfer the bike and keep the money. By the time my companion arrived and we extricated ourselves, 114 eyes watched us, four of them crossed.

On the bus trip to Lahore, the flying infestation continued, and wipers-against-glass did a poor job of separating wings from thorax and head. Our driver and his buddy played a game of overtaking each other until one agitated passenger stepped partway into the aisle and blurted out "Saf-i-ty first!"

In Lahore Tom and I had a falling-out, partly a result of what might be called my wanderbust. I recovered thanks to a bath and bed graciously provided by a daughter of the Fosters. After a reunion on the platform near the evening train to India, we signed a treaty and rolled across a perilous line that divided Punjab from Punjab.

On the Indian side we began a tour apparently based on the theme of Earthly Materials. **Gold: Religion.** The Sikh temple in Amritsar rose from a reflecting pool where I took off my shoes and socks and waded. (About this week I began pulling the heel-holes to the top of my foot.) **Brick: War.** The massive Red Fort was now stormed by monkeys that scampered about with little appreciation for the Mughals of the 1600s. **Marble: Love.** A white mausoleum, the Taj Mahal, separated heaven from earth by onion domes and minarets.

At the train station there in Agra, the second-class waiting room became our hotel. We had just climbed into our rumple-stuffed bags when Tom spied a "big mouse" prowling around; the next morning he reported that it had stared at him during the night, and I found holes in the pockets of my jacket and pants. As an extreme contrast between mammals, elephants lent regalia-clad gravitas to the Republic Day parade in New Delhi, January 26, 1962.

The sunny, mild weather now blessed us with a touch of the imagined Ceylon. The landscape was spacious and green, dotted with villages and water buffalo. We tacitly gave up the banana-eating contest after more than a hundred between us and switched to a suntan duel. Tom remembers that in one city we were very thirsty, and the cool carrot juice was the best drink he's ever had—"But the sugar cane was less like eating than gnawing on a tree branch." In the city of Lucknow we poked around a dusty outdoor market where I bought a paperback copy of *Camille*, by Dumas; the boudoir of its tubercular heroine became a refuge disturbed only by her coughing. At a hotel I turned over my pillow to discover a cache of twenty-seven dollars worth of rupees, a sum that I wired to the owner, who sent me a note of gratitude.

In Benares one cobra rose from wicker prison, one from clay jail. And a troupe of necklace-jingling gypsies, hardened and skilled, danced for cash. That night we took a path along the river: above us towered temples and pilgrim shelters, grotesquely silhouetted; below us wide cement steps, or ghats, for pilgrims who immersed themselves in the holy Ganges. We could hear the hubbub of the city and could make out the grand curve of the water by the lights that crowded to its edge.

"I wonder what these big fires are for," said Tom. We watched a man poke one of the six blazes with a long stick. "They're not for heat," he mused. "They're not for fuel."

"Look at these!" I exclaimed, pointing to two stretchers that dipped into the river and held silk-wrapped bodies.

"This is a crematorium," replied Tom quietly. Abashed, we made our way through the narrow city passageways, almost getting run down by four chanting stretcher-carriers. That night living mummies helped to fill the three-level racks of our departing train. It rumbled over the bridge across the same don't-dip-a-toe-in-it river to which they had made a pilgrimage. For us, however, Doomsday failed to arrive despite the predictions: *Ashtagraha*, conjunction of eight planets, had held the area in its grips for a month.

Next day in a warm, crowded train car, a spider crawled near my neck, but as I reached up to smash it, a passenger gently restrained my wrist: "That is one of the things that Gandhi taught us." ("Teach *him,* spider!" I prayed.) Rails ran out of southeast at Calcutta, where on the teeming streets an occasional child sought charity because of his distended scrotum, a parentally-induced affliction. I hired a bicycle rickshaw and felt a little embarrassed to have some fellow bent over and pumping pedals for a stock boy. Cows wandered among streetcars, victims of their own holiness.

We had reached Longitude 88 E, where one more step would turn Going to Coming. Now my father was driving to work while I ate curry for dinner, and the grandfather's clock, its pendulum un-stayed for a night's sleep, was able to gong galore at Bengal midnight.

Amrita Bazar Patrika, February 4, 1962.

14. The Estate IV: "World Ball"

Marge and I would drum our knuckles on the glass and yell at the plump, hairy animal. For it was in the herb garden sharing our basil, rosemary, parsley, and mint. Sometimes when we opened the basement door, the critter would dart down the hill to its hidden burrow. Mixed feelings: we admired its self-reliant distance-keeping, and we regretted its vulnerability to dogs. But we also objected to the chew-marks on the door of the shed, and once Marge reported that "Groundy is up to no good" near the barn. Once, unimpressed with the approaching car, it departed with reluctance. We were actually relieved when it reappeared after the winter, but was this *our* woodchuck? "You can tell by its sweet breath," said Marge.

Eventually rabbits also appeared to twitch-nibble here and there without danger of ending up in a pie like Peter's father. One afternoon I flung off the cover of the barbecue grill and found myself staring into the dark eyes of a field mouse that stood shaking in terror. I myself was startled by its human-like reaction, and the creature seemed more anthropomorphic than any Mickey. I intended to whisper "Sorry" but it was gone. Months later it ventured back to chew a hole in the leather work-coat that covered the cistern pump during a frost.

Near the shed in front of the basement door stretched a thin, glossy strip of new tire a yard long. Or was it an oversize strand of licorice? We halted in admiration and watched it ripple slowly away in the direction of its flicking black tongue. So the snake charmed *us*. A more positive encounter than Fred's when he came upon a blacksnake with two pairs of eyes, one of them a frog's.

"Rand!" whispered Marge, "come quick." We tiptoed onto the screen porch and she pointed at the gutter over the stairs: clinging to it upside down were tiny legs. Gone the next day, perhaps able to squeeze in with the crowd upstairs. Although these flying mammals caught insects with their nocturnal wing-nets, bugs in turn caught bats. A few such parasites lay around dead or dying on the floor, probably dispatched by chemicals that the exterminator had aimed at flies and Asian lady beetles, *Harmonia axyridis* (Pallas), of which there are about 5,000 species. Marge hit the upstairs window frame, *Wham! Wham!* in an attempt to evict the suspended-upside-down squatters from their daylight home between logs and trim. As evening fell on the deck, pieces of trim around one of the triangular windows detached themselves and zipped away as a black flapping.

I decided to extend our yard to the trucked-in gray birch. Although the mower was advertised as self-propelled, the self was your author. Leaning into it, I jabbed out a circle from the even taller tall weeds around the papery trunk. Clack-a-crunch! The engine stopped. I pulled back the mower and looked down to see—what was it? A manufactured object? An integument? I remembered decades earlier when the rotary blade had made garter-snake purée, but this shred of hide was too broad.

Then I perceived claws and the corner of a shell around a scrap of red flesh. I was mortified and a bit sickened. Had I known. As time passed, I wondered if I should tell Sidney about this ill-fated turtle. I did want him to understand that what I called the World-Ball rolls in nasty stuff. Finally I decided to risk erring on the side of truth rather than of prolonged innocence. His reaction was a distress that included repeated demands for explanation. Feeling bad but not wrong, I still felt guilty about sacrificing wildlife for esthetics. A year later when I spotted an intact dome on the grass, I gratefully admired its hieratic inscriptions, then watched the animal's neck rise from its grassy snack and its left eye regard my greeting with hauteur.

Deer sometimes favored us with a tableau of browsers. With their wiry toughness, did they not resemble the offspring of mules and greyhounds? Every few seconds they looked up in tail-switching vigilance, their ears horizontal as if pulled by marionette strings. With a start they'd run off as if bounding over the moon with its gravity five-sixths of the earth's. Or they'd stay put on the graveled lane and look at our car as if wondering "What year Subaru is that?" Or they would scatter haplessly before it in daylight, dusk, or dark.

The proliferation of this species was largely the result of humans, who had killed off their predators (especially wolves) and created an ideal environment of woods-bordered spaces. Fred and Ann had to construct a fence around their vegetables that prevented the deepest dig-under or the highest jump-over and that lacked only guard towers. One writer reviewed findings about the deer's threat to agriculture and declared that "doing one's own killing [is] the most ecologically responsible way to live."**(1)** When our visitors from South Carolina shot a buck and dragged it uphill to a trailer, I imagined the animal's last words: "You can't hunt on Sunday!"

A buzz of flying stingers caused Marge to scrutinize the restored branches of the deer-chewed cypress. She discovered a puffed pastry with teeth inside to eat itself: a hornets' nest with rows of tiny combs. "It reminds me of corn-on-the-cob." Because she was at risk for an allergic reaction, a stream of poison was shot from a distance before you could say *anaphylaxis.*

One day I sat on a bench lubricating my work-boots with a rag-full of neatsfoot oil, the rich smell taking me back to our childhood basement with its shelf of cans. I would never leave boots outside for fear they would shelter a spider, especially one that's husband-nourished. Then into view came a daddy-longlegs that prospected around the floor of the carport. When the white tuft of a thistle rolled at him, he sashayed gracefully around it, reminding me of Gulliver and some close call in the land of the Brobdingnagians. Insects found our place uninviting, though, because we had established a sort of chemical moat that was filled by a guy with a canister.

In the nearby sandbox, my visiting brother Cap sculpted a large turtle for Sidney—complete with beak, flippers, tail, and inscribed shell. But when I peeled back the plastic cover another day, a colony of ants scrambled to transport little white things out of the sunlight. "Eggs," said Marge. Slugs, orange and moist, festooned dirt on the edge of the boards and rubbed their eyes at the glare. Upon the cool skin of a toad I laid a finger and invited my grandson to do the same.

Whenever we tromped around outside, we had to reckon with bloodsucking acarid arachnids (easier to say "ticks"). Our means of defense included sprays, intimate inspections, and tweezers. Again we regarded the deer with some apprehension. "Rats on stilts" is what Fred called them, and flea-bearing rats have a negative public-health record, so we had to be wary of Lyme Disease, what I'll call the Bambonic plague.

"A calipitter!" exclaimed Sid. Indeed, a turgid, green, articulated tube crawled along a fieldstone step in a rare conjunction of animal, vegetable, and mineral. As I looked out the window, a moth skittered up and down and around the pane, only to quit trying to get into the reflected outside. As for monarch butterflies with their delicate orange pennants that flap in their own wind—our carpenter enjoyed telling me that they love dog feces. Information I could have done without. It rubbed my face in the risk of investing nature with comforting notions such as Mother Earth, my Father's World, Wakan Tanka, the still, sad music of humanity—even dear Gaia. Nature, wasps-and-all.

We produced our first batch of kitchen compost and spread it around Marge's flower garden. Much of it had spent the winter frozen in a plastic drum. Handfuls of clay had merged with vegetable scraps, shrimp tails, eggshells, the odd tortilla, and novel coffee blends that joined Costa-Malan: Suma-Temala, Ethio-Lumbian, and Rwa-wiian. From a second batch we got only enough to feed the Atlas blue cedar, itself of North African origin.

I finished hauling brown dirt from the trucked-in hill behind the pole barn to shallow places in the yard. Because the hill-climbing, shovel-wielding, and barrow-pushing made my knees hurt, I limited myself to six loads a day. Once I was proud of myself for not adding one more load, two at most, but then I bought four 50-pound bags of denatured cow manure, hauled them from the car, and spread them around the filled places. More exercise came when the wind tumbled empty plastic bags down the ridge without catching on the spines of a hawthorn bush.

I hauled water, too, from well to tree via the kitchen sink. Before washing the dishes, I would turn on the "hot" spigot and catch the flow in a kettle until the water warmed up. Then I would carry the vessel outside—preventing a spill with the collaboration of eyes, spindles, Golgis, butt, and a screen door that Tom had rigged to stay open. I would favor the pencil-holly, or the twice-transplanted blue spruce, or the conical evergreen called a "dwarf-something," a name ill-suited to a gigantic carbon sponge.

Because of the chronic near-drought, we bought an above-ground cistern that collected rainwater from the gutters. It was almost as tall as I was and as wide as my outstretched arms. A chain of hoses from the pump in the carport let me water all the trees we had lowered as root-balls—indeed, as an incipient arboretum. Pretending to be a storm, I made thunder-noise to entertain Marge (at least the first time). Once as the hose lay in a straight line down the gravel, its shadow somehow undulated a couple feet away—a puzzle solved when I recognized it as a trail of water that had dribbled from the nozzle.

The cover of the cistern—dislodged. By an animal? The wind? A forgetful husband (my partner's theory)? I wrestled it on after balancing my way along a half-wall of concrete blocks and leaning over a space onto the sloped top of the cylinder. Later I remembered how we had left our grandson unattended long enough for him to fill a seed-and-dirt jar with hose water instead of leaving it moist. Contacted over the phone, Sidney asked, "Did I put it back right?"

One morning I opened a faucet to sputter. So all weekend we had to carry the precious liquid from both grocery store and above-ground cistern. We lost sleep over the water supply of Floyd County, notoriously hidden and zig-zag in amid the underlying karst, the basement of basements. We hoped for a broken pump. Failing that, a deepened well or a second one to be drilled in a lucky spot. (Randall with dowser's twig was Randall with Alzheimer's.) Without a water supply, our house was like our motor home without gasoline. The rescue-chariot arrived first thing Monday morning in the guise of an uncompromisingly workaday truck. A pump-and-well expert tested the electric current in the basement and at the pump, both of which sparked obediently. Therefore was the well sand-sucking dry? He apologized for the next step as being rather primitive: holding a small rock over the pipe, he let it go, and after two or three seconds.... *Splash!*

Another water problem continued: none from the sky. Then in the middle of the night I heard a gentle sound. Don't get your hopes up, probably just the ceiling fan. I cocked my ears toward the open window and made out a steady pitter. Ahhh. In the morning "I went outside to move one of the hoses," reported Marge, "and heard the sound of drops on my raincoat." We drank in the view of Dodd Creek Valley, vaporous white as if from snow. And to the north, across the hill-hidden Rt. 221 and down the tree-crowded hill, mist glided to our left, with several little peaks that seemed to issue from hot springs or a waterfall.

In winter we retirees took a late-afternoon hike to the farmer's end of Annie Lane through a tunnel of snow-bent pines. The sky-cover was dissipating and in the southwest, against pale hues, clouds whipped like smoke. The blaze itself was a yellow disk upon a hill that doesn't even exist in the leafy summer. Another hike revealed imprints of animal wandering, especially holes that I peered deep into and saw two-toed impressions lined by blue shadows. What about that odd pattern atop the white? "A wing-dragger" explained our friend Dennis.

Shortly after walking on the icy flakes with Sidney, Marge returned with a bloody scrape on one side of her nose. Shaken but grateful to have all bones intact, she forbade me to venture out. Nevertheless, he and I soon tested different modes of treading—in snow or in now-frozen boot-tracks, each kind a challenge that he enjoyed. I tried to pull him over the surface by holding his arm, but he twirled and fell, then did the same on purpose.

He wore a thick jacket, red mittens, and a knitted hat that represented a dinosaur, although sparkling hazel eyes below the yarn-line diminished the threat. We set out on a quest to reach the pasture fence and a special tree. Although we tried to follow the outline-encrusted ice-prints, whenever I shifted my booted weight onto the snow, it gave way in two or three rapid crunches. I held one of Sidney's hands as he pointed with the other to a boulder partway down the side of the ridge, screened by brush, darkly wet, a symbol in need of a novel. Happily we labored on, chatting. "Where are the cows?" "Maybe inside." A couple of times I pointed to the fence 'way through the trees, and we finally reached the end of the path. "Look for the tree with things hanging from it." With my help he made out the random, long, skinny brown bean-pods that hung toward the snow. I pulled one off, then lifted him so he could do the same with a grin.

Trudging back, we stopped a few times so the lad could poke at some snow-ice and offer me a bite of it, again beaming: "What kind of ice cream could we make?" By the time we reached home, the boy was in my arms and the souvenir in my pocket, although by then the husk had fallen open and the inner string had unraveled. A handbook identified the tree as a catalpa (family *Bignoniaceae*), which in my mind would become a locust by the time I trespassed in Colorado.

At random times a baleful sound echoed from a cow-path somewhere on the opposite hill. A prolonged "Woe," it suggested the animal's intimation of its beefly fate. An occasional abrupt bellow, on the other hand, issued a threat to cow-dom. And at the extreme of belligerence, the air was once split by a trumpeting elephant, or by a long-vanished megafauna, that announced its tusk-out from the ground, which it now pitched off violently as clumps and rocks.

One day the hooves of a burly intruder stopped short in the yard. The animal stared, maybe testing our reaction, maybe expressing hesitation or defiance. We clapped, it mooed, and the half-grown steer galloped back toward the farm. We never did see a bear, unlike Dennis, who found one lounging in the tent he uses as a wildlife-observation blind.

A half-grown cat wandered onto the grounds, someone's responsibility and now nobody's and everybody's. In the frigid darkness it meowed plaintively and hobbled because of a bum rear-leg. I clapped it away. No pets allowed. We travel too often, we abhor song-less feather-piles, and we already had a pair of guards—carved shishi-dog bookends given to me by Cap as a souvenir of Okinawa. The creature made forays toward the house and dart-limped away. I telephoned the animal control department but got no interest.

Out came a dish of milk, which brought a tentative approach followed by a meow and the sound of lapping. When I hoisted up the stray, it was like an empty fur purse. I began to warm the milk and soon mixed it with Half & Half. The cat would follow me around. Once as I carried its purring and increasing weight, a riled-up barking caused it to leap out of my arms and race to its bundle of towels on the covered barbecue grill. Then we sheltered it in the pole barn in an upholstered box near an electric heater, where our dependent seemed comfy even though its bowl of water froze. To Sidney I explained that the ice would melt from heat and asked if he knew where this energy would come from. When he drew a blank, we stepped outside and I pointed toward satin tucks in the clouds; he went back in, got the bowl, and set it outside.

Marge and I were grateful to the Humane Society for organizing a group excursion to the vet's that included a gift-pack of stitches, and grateful to the Cat Lady for arranging an adoption after five weeks. Despite repeated explanations, Sidney could not absorb the animal's disappearance: "That's the pole barn where Tuxedo isn't."

From one edge of the cold celestial glass of the heavens to the other ran a smear. Marge deemed it the Milky Way, but I scoffed, attributing it to some kind of a rogue cloud. Raising binoculars I almost staggered at the sight, the impossible carbonated galaxy. Another night we studied the horizon in search of an imminent lunar eclipse. As we gave up and started to turn away—had one of us noted something? That dim eeriness… in line with a cluster of amber street-lights across the valley…. Rounded like the tip of a fingernail, it now seemed alive, to move, to grow higher and bigger. In a few moments it revealed itself as a red-orange egg with one half darkly concave, the negative of the earth's curve.

At other times the moon surprised me as to when or where it would appear. At least I was more informed than little Andrea when she had pointed from over my shoulder and exclaimed, "A moon." Of course I understood that the sun doesn't rise, that the earth turns again to reveal it. Still, wanting our grandson to have a better awareness than mine about the earth's nightly upside-down spin, I gave a little talk on the World Ball. As for the earth's spherical shape, I had earned an almost kinesthetic feel for it.

But why does one season give way to another? Not many people understand the reason for the seasons (apology to Christmas constables), so here is an explanation:
- Hold an apple with the stem upright (i.e., the North Pole).
- Stand facing a lamp (the sun).
- Tilt the apple toward a point on the opposite side of the lamp. The top of the apple will now lean closest to the lamp-sun. (It's June 21, summer solstice in the Northern Hemisphere—longest day.)

- Start walking around the lamp—but keep the apple tilted *toward that same point*. Do not swivel it in an attempt to keep it tilted toward the circumference of the walking-circle.
- When you get halfway around the lamp, the North-Pole-stem will be inclined farthest away from the apple-earth. (Winter solstice in the Northern Hemisphere.)
- When you return to the starting point, the tilted stem is once again closest to the bulb-sun.

Of course to trace this seasonal pattern there is no need to spin the apple 365 ¼ times. Halfway positions in the circle represent the fall and spring equinoxes, when the stem is tilting neither toward nor away from the lamp: sunrise to sunset, sunset to sunrise, twelve hours each. To help develop a proprio-celestial feel for this annual Tilt-a-Whirl, lean toward a point and walk in a circle sans apple.

In June the morning blazed into the dining room from the northeast-left; by December the sun was getting a tan in Miami. On the twenty-first I vowed to witness the advent of the shortest day, but the sky was unable to throw off its gray blanket. I had given up when the world began to lighten, slowly yet quickly. A hint of rays revealed patches of thin cloud that streamed toward the southeast as if being sucked into a vortex. For a while Marge and I stood peering at the glow through branches naked or needled. Was that hump a mountain or a cloudbank? Taking out the binoculars, we looked through desultory snowflakes at what seemed to be a luminous reflection without a source. I had pretty much conceded that this was the best we could hope for when—"Look, Rand, there it is!" Through two lenses and between two pines blazed the top of the far-swinging disk.

One night the temperature fell to 10 degrees as silver clouds rushed in from the north beneath the moon. The hum of the blower on the woodstove, a supplement to propane, could not muffle the roaring wind, and we could feel it try to jimmy the kitchen window. So I stuffed the perimeter with foam rubber pads, a piece of cardboard, and a long, green scarf. Later when I couldn't find my gloves, I realized they were part of the weatherizing combo. Remarked Fred about an emailed photograph: "You guys pull out all the stops when it comes to professional insulation—not to mention pillow stuffing, beach towels & the mattress pad from grandma's bed."

Icicles that braided the deck-railing melted to the wires underneath that were dotted with colored bulbs, mementos of Christmas. In the woods Marge enjoined me not to tread on the very ice I intended to whack from the firs, and this time I obeyed. As wet drops plummeted and the temperature edged above freezing, the evergreens gradually threw off subjection; their branches unbent and even flounced a little in the wind. The pencil holly, having earlier collapsed under ice into a pile of green shavings, could once again be held between a thumb and finger raised inside a bedroom window.

On the deck the wet planks gave no hint of the two-foot drifts that we had recently tossed off in stages. "I love to shovel snow!" Marge had declared as she burst into the house with rosy cheeks. "I would make a game of it—I wanted to see how far I could throw the next shovel and just see if I could get farther over each time." But this strenuous chore pinched a nerve in my boyhood memory, and I vowed never to hire anyone else to do it.

Once I took an axe to chop ice and snow in front of the pole-barn doors with an axe, then shoveled off the chunks, to hasten melting and gain traction for the RV. The exercise felt good for the first half hour, but I swung, bent, and hefted so much that the next day Marge had to take extra spells of driving as we motor-homed to the Deep South.

Warm in Florida we moseyed along the St. John's River on the *Penelope,* a pleasure-tugboat owned by the Hollinger family. By contrast to the long-ago river cruise taken by a pair of vagabonds, I no longer bummed cigarettes and my friend was captain. Now we puttered southward in quest of spring, whiling away the hours amiably and celebrating my sixty-ninth birthday.

Upon our return to the slushy Virginia hill, we learned that two more snowfalls had kept people isolated. A woman in Marge's church reported that she hadn't been into town for so long, she'd forgotten how to talk. Once again a long white cushion swelled over the deck, matte in the shade of an afternoon already two-thirds of the way to the vernal equinox. To speed the melting process in front of the pole barn, I shovel-scraped a prone angel in front of the double doors so they would swing open thanks to a pair of negatives.

Whooosh becomes whistle-and-groan as flakes speed past horizontally. At the creak of a beam I almost expect the cabin to roll and pitch as wind from decades earlier seems to whip salty droplets through the rigging of the HMS *Nova Scotia*. The great waves bowl us to starboard, and the deck leans back into the valley before the next wave threatens to o'ertop us. To keep my glasses on I hold a rubber band attached to one plastic bow. With Tom and a girl from Canada I stand next to the railing and watch the big ones roll in. We yell over the gale and then weave all over the deck in search of vantage points. Standing askew, our hair flying in every which way, we laugh at each other when into the railing we stumble. That night we watch the glimmer of a lighthouse, probably off Newfoundland, the only thing visible except for the white foam. The beam descends far below us… then slowly rises, up, up, up into where the sky would be. "As high as the moon!" someone screams. Then down it plunges like a falling star.

Footnote:
1. Jim Minick, *Finding a Clear Path.* Morgantown, WV: Vandalia Press, zoos, p. 53.

15. Rapunzel: The Child for the Plant

"Look at that neat tower," exclaimed my spouse. "It reminds me of Rapunzel!" She was driving to the grocery store with our grandson, and they passed an old brown-brick silo with a conical, cedar-shingled top that held a small dormer window.

"Rapunzel, Rapunzel, who's that?" Gigi was unable to remember the tale well, so she drove to the library and took out a volume by that name. Written and illustrated by Paul O. Zelinsky, it combines features of several literary versions, including that of the Grimm brothers' (itself influenced by earlier stories). His paintings are inspired by those of the Italian Renaissance—with its relish for color and light, garments with shape and weight, facial expressions, accurate anatomy, and naturalistic perspective (*Wikipedia*). To leaf through the volume is to understand why its cover bears the golden Caldecott Medal.**(1)**

In one respect the painter literally turns earth to art. Although he used some synthetic pigments, "There was a lot of raw sienna and raw umber, basically the dirt of Siena and Umbria, uncooked." (All quotations refer to private correspondence with Mr. Zelinsky, 2011). He also used Naples Yellow, one of his favorites before it was declared toxic.

And with this art, the writer-painter in turn graces the earth.

From the open window, indirect sunshine promises a bright future and helps render the couple beatific. This first illustration shows the smiling, clasping parents-to-be as they intertwine their fingers on the woman's belly. Her robe is the hue of an apricot, perhaps another reason this scene might be called *Testing for Ripeness*.

Ominously the landscape in the next picture, the garden of a sorceress, looks closed in. It ends at a high wall that the sun brightens without touching the plants directly. Such vegetation is doubly confined because it is pruned, espalier-ed, bonsai-d, and otherwise manipulated into designs. A couple of them resemble green snowmen-guards, topiaries that may even hint at bewitched human beings. This kind of reduction also characterizes two statues, humans estheticized. One is a marble mother—warm only in sunshine—who stands holding a baby that will never squall or get a new tooth. A lizard prowls the grounds as a cold-blooded version of a cat. Even the base of the fountain is walled by a short octagon.

The sorceress has a cousin-in-enclosing, MacMurtrey, the protagonist of another superbly illustrated book. "With thick, coarse hands, [he] captured every bird, caged every beast, and fenced in the hills and every tree upon them." Still unhappy, he declared,

"I will build a wall to cage the sea." Homunculi are merely spectators on the periphery until they end up rescuing him from death and egomania.(2) But the sorceress remains immured in her character.

The only human being visible in her courtyard gazes through the same open window into the garden. This living mother-to-be desires some of the rapunzel plant—i.e., the rampion, which the author defines as a flower with an edible leaf and tuberous root (Zelinsky 1997). Her husband must climb down into the garden because there is no access by door or window. The purloined salad causes the woman a mind-altering experience— an almost sexual reaction that is uncongenial to the repressive garden. This plant becomes even more menacing when she says she'll die without another batch.

As the husband kneels again at the blossoms, the sorceress leans over him and spreads her arms and cloak like a grimacing anti-angel. Her offer: the child for the plant. A diptych follows, unaccompanied by words. Its left panel shows the still-recumbent mother, pale, her orange hair faded, along with the midwife and the seated father. He can barely watch as (on its right panel) the sorceress tilts her face close to the baby's in an almost sacrilegious parody of Madonna and Child, then bears Rapunzel past her own cradle, empty-fancy, into the sunlit doorway.(3)

Does Rapunzel faintly echo the Eden story in Genesis? Both tell of a wife who eats a prohibited plant and who enlists her husband as a co-conspirator. Both tell of punishment for disobedience, and by exile— Adam and Eve from the garden, and the later Rapunzel into the wilderness. Jehovah and the sorceress are gardeners who set limits on human beings, one by a command, the other by an enclosure. The male is a divine figure described as a human being, the female as a human being with magical powers. Jehovah forbids his creatures to understand good and evil because he wants them to remain in a state of innocence, while the sorceress regards human beings only as a threat to her possessions— one of which becomes Rapunzel. Mr. Zelinsky, however, surmises that the woman partly intended to keep the child innocent. Rich ambiguity: one power of art.

Both of these powerful figures—deity and sorceress—resemble single parents. In the next illustration the latter perverts maternal love by working her needlepoint while the forfeited girl dances outside like a daughter of the prelapsarian Adam and Eve. The pond and river in nearby paintings exemplify as well as symbolize the freedom she will lose. The Stepmother, as Rapunzel calls her, evidently feels her anti-growth impulse renewed, for she drags her charge through the woods as if from puberty. Especially because the captor is no sorcerer (male), her motivation seems to have little to do with the erotic and everything with the emotionally sclerotic.

She now even perverts the life-enhancing power of art by building a marble keep, magnificent in height, engineering, and décor. The campanile's design-segments suggest the bars of a prison or the stripes of a prisoner's uniform. Lavender petals top the base and clash with the geometric facade and hexagonal shape—flowers transformed to architectural decoration, somewhat like the girl herself, who now serves as its focal point. In the next image the designer uses her physical prowess not to create anything but instead to visit her possession like a miser tending a gold-hoard. She scales the tower with grotesque gymnastics, her only instrument Rapunzel's hair, a gorgeous, luxuriant, and lively sign of growth—carrot-top indeed.

The story does not touch on the damage wrought upon someone who is mentally and socially foot-bound. Held in near-solitary confinement—even a premature sepulcher—she stays unchanged, uncomplaining, and beautiful, not to mention elegant.**(4)** Although a human being, she has a kinship with the plant that saved her life and supplied her name. Conceived in the spring, she reveals touches of a fertility-spirit, and the tower may suggest a lofty root-cellar that holds dormant life. As another hint of her close association with nature, she sings to the birds, a vocalization emphasized because her words are quoted only once, elsewhere in the text. It is her artistic impulse—rather than her invisible person—that first charms the Prince. In this tale, unlike "Snow White" or "Sleeping Beauty," the heroine is the enchantress.

The Prince climbs upward in a reversal of the direction taken by Rapunzel's trespassing father. For the first time, the young woman beholds a man, as does Miranda in *The Tempest*, isolated by father and island. This new character's royal status, following convention, is a means of idealizing him. Luckily he behaves like a prince of a fellow, so his kindness overcomes her fear. The two eventually conduct a brief ceremony that solemnizes their relationship.

One day the gray-haired woman understands why Rapunzel's dress has become tight. Although the text reports her anger, the painting also suggests fear. She is the most complex character, fraught with contradiction and unknowable motivation. Wicked with Issues. She is also a classy dresser who disdains the unimaginative black garb of the witch in favor of dark green. (Terre verte—i.e. green earth, a mixture of minerals—"is one of the main components of her green gown," writes the artist.) The formal setting of inlaid floor and ornate table set in relief the lunging sorceress and the backward-leaning Rapunzel, their robes in turmoil.

In the next, two-page scene the older woman, eyes crazy-wide, hair gray against orange, snips off the offending tresses while the girl cups her hands around her temples and squeezes her eyes shut. Both figures lean out of the tower onto its dizzying view. In the distance, near the center of the overwhelming, desolate, waterless landscape sits the tiny figure of Rapunzel. This leaf is a proleptic view of her expulsion, which will trade enclosure for exposure. She eventually gives birth to twins, a hint that to stifle nature is to redouble it.

Meanwhile the blithely ignorant prince climbs the rope of hair again only to be shocked by a figure of wrinkled, vindictive, and sarcastic fury. His humanity is emphasized when it is his grief, not her push, that causes him to let go and plummet to the ground. He survives at the cost of his eyesight. After wandering through the land with a cane, he hears the familiar voice and rushes toward his dear wife. Their reunion is painted with such boulder-tilting and costume-swirling energy that the image appears almost cinematic. To the artist (personal communication) this and the birth scene are like bookends: each is a two-page spread devoid of text, with the exit of the baby-swaddling sorceress concluding one segment and beginning the next, which is climaxed by the reunion of Rapunzel and her husband.

When Rapunzel embraces the prince, she sheds two tears into his eyes and restores his sight. This is magic of her own, twins again, a hint that human love can be medicinal. The drops invite comparison with the spittle that Jesus mixed with dirt to anoint the eyes of a blind man (John 9:6). Yet they offer warm and salty reminders that this tale is secular.

It elevates the generous instinct to bear fruit over the selfish one to prevent or constrain it—procreation over proprietorship. Love is not divine but instead earthly, both fecund and healing. Unlike the Eden story, Zelinsky's *Rapunzel* does not prize obedience, nor does it view human beings as wretches—unless cruelly mistreated.

No angels are agencies. They never affect the plot, comfort the imprisoned Rapunzel (who never prays), sacralize her erotic contact with the Prince, wing her way to a reunion, or assure her parents as to anyone's safety in this world or bliss in the hereafter. None of Humperdinck's fourteen sentimental angels appear. Phony euphony: they can sing a lullaby but not keep children out of the oven, a job for Gretel's wit.

Neither story, *Rapunzel* or Genesis, casts much light on iniquity. The latter provides an unsatisfying explanation for human failings, viciousness, and suffering by blaming Eve and Adam. Their transgression can actually be admired as intellectual curiosity, however, by someone who craves the rampion of thought. Certainly their punishment can be regarded as disproportionate to their error. *Rapunzel,* in a different sort of limitation, cloaks everything bad in the sorceress.

The final painting is a tableau of the family in affectionate repose, the father's arm behind the mother, whose own arm curves down to touch one of the orange-haired children. With its heart-warming conclusion, the book (like its sources) eschews any reminder that the heroine no longer has parents and the twins have no grandparents. The tableau, however, might be imagined as the left half of a diptych; the right half pictures a husband and wife, gray of hair and mien, who tend a cobwebbed cradle.

In our correspondence, Mr. Zelinsky mused upon the tale's stock, upbeat ending. It would be too incongruous, he observed, if the story involved actual people. But the narrative is art rather than life. It does not offer a moral even though it describes "persevering and life going on" for both the prince and his bride. Yet as with other fairy- and folk-tales (like the better ones of the Grimm brothers), the very weirdness of the clashing tones is appealing. "Things happen, and then other things happen. Get used to it, and declare a happy ending with what you've got."

Footnotes:

1. *Rapunzel*. New York: Dutton Children's Books, 1997. The Caldecott Medal "is awarded annually by the Association for Library Service to Children, a division of the American Library Association, to the artist of the most distinguished American picture book for children" (ALA/ALSC Caldecott Medal Home Page).
2. Marc Sutherland, *MacMurtrey's Wall*. New York: Abrams, 2001.
3. "I think that maybe the rapunzel planting was a setup," reports the author-illustrator, "and the sorceress actually wanted the baby all along." As for the statues—one woman with a stick and another with a child—they "make sense given who the sorceress is and what she thinks about." Regarding the tower she later constructs, he calls the sorceress "an artist, a very good draftsman." He sees her as wanting to recapture her own youth and feels that she does not intend for Rapunzel to suffer.
4. This drive to control someone radically, described in "A Rose for Emily," informs *The Collector*, a novel by John Fowles (1963). After Louis XIV revoked the Edict of Nantes in 1685, 130 Protestant women were confined for the rest of their lives in the Tower of Constance, Aigues-Mortes (www.museedudesert.com).

16. The Estate V: Free of Earth, Bound to It

Oriental bittersweet (*Celastrus orbiculatus*) had crossed the Pacific in a flowerpot. This vine became Korean kudzu. It threatened to woody-perennialize the land, and upon reaching The Estate, it mounted trees as staging areas for its assault on the cabin. I tried to cut the twisters while negotiating a steep incline crowded with thorn-stalks, pine branches, wild grapevines and galax, but I had to call up General Landscaper and his Hispanic mercenaries.

Later I did more reconnaissance along the other side of the old logging trail and down the hill. Spotting a grapevine in the canopy of a small maple, I cut and yanked it with the long-handled pruner, leaving some biomass to hang like an oxbow lake of foliage. Then I spied a narrow, twisted artery on the trunk. Extending long-handled loppers I leaned over the incline, stretched out my arms, aimed, and pulled the handles together to cut—air. I remembered a story called "The Most Dangerous Game," where the protagonist reaches for his dropped pipe and falls overboard.**(1)** Grateful for the warning, I smiled confidently, leaned an inch more, and became free of earth.

Down the slope I plunged in utter helplessness, limbs useless, able only to wonder about what else might come as I watched my safety glasses plow the scruff. I stopped short, probably after ramming into the very tree I had been attending. Chakras joggled, afraid for my hurting neck, I managed to get to my knees, retrieve the red loppers, straggle up the bank, find the pruner, and make my way to the cabin. Although my eyesight was intact, my forehead and nose were cut and abraded, and the wide-brimmed hat that Tom had given me displayed a bloody spot.

"A little skid mark," said Marge. "Looks like you've had a difficult delivery. With forceps." For a day or two my whole body was sore, and for several weeks my neck drew a yell when I turned it while looking down. I emailed news of this misadventure to a number of people, some of whom laced their concern with wit. Tom: "I doubt that the hat was safety tested for that use." Richard: "Bad things always happen when we try to do something under conditions of cold sobriety." Cap: "Be advised that the family name is Wells, not Wallenda."

Again the earthly stem-pole tilts away from the star-lamp. Flakes scatter under a strangely blue sky, wafting, spiraling, dipping, falling, rising, jerking as if to evade a predator, swooping down to the snow-pile or down and back up, some frantically trying to migrate back to their northern origin, a few approaching the window of the glass door, where one sticks momentarily. The whistling varies between two pitches, one of them with a shrill overtone, as the flakes shoot past the tall hardwood trunks on the opposite hill. More creaking as the superstructure bends. Again a toneless hum, then another whistling note. Clouds slide down the pale blue sky behind the nearby hardwood crowns, which bob gently or sway, each in its own rhythm, each branch and twig silhouetted as it seems to poke out of Storkers Knob a mile or two in the background.

The hardwoods being leafless, I took advantage of the afternoon rays that slanted down from the southeast; training binoculars onto the uphill evergreens to the northeast, I hoped to discern the brown-brick Rapunzel-silo, but nary a shingle. "Invisible," I thought, but not imaginary."

One night we were besieged by the fiercest wind since Hurricane Hugo split the pines around us throughout the South Carolina night. Because of the roar we decided to sleep in the basement bedroom, which is windowless and protected by earthworks. Becoming too warm under the comforter and next to the heater, I re-climbed two sets of stairs and lay as the roof tried to hold up and as the building, its profile a liability on a ridge, swayed.

Once as Marge and I hiked up the lane, she exclaimed, "The tree is gone!" At this nonsensical idea I scanned the field and yard but saw nothing amiss. "The dead trunk," she added. I now looked at emptiness where the bottom half, still tall, had offered both perch and home-hole. I remembered pushing it and feeling a slight give while craning upward to see which way to bolt.

Spring paid another visit, as did our grandson. When he picked up a handful of 57 and set them next to the driveway, Gigi asked him why. "So they'll turn into dirt." In a more promising venture we scattered flower-seeds. The little guy rode uphill and down in the red wheelbarrow, smiling and holding tight atop the bags of store-bought compost, one per trip. We mixed the three into the brown dirt that I had wheeled to declivities. Two-toed tracks punctuated several of the older and muddy patches, causing me to remind Sidney of our winter's trek in the snow. Luckily we finished before the gray rumbling brought more than a few raindrops. Gigi, pleased that we had enjoyed our venture so much, gave Sid a bath but unenthusiastically swept Black Kow off the stairs.

In July our vegetable garden matured as a flower, leaves, and vine— with one acorn squash—all from kitchen compost spread around a transplanted gingko tree. Marge's practiced fingers estimated its diameter as 10 cm and tape-measured it as 9.5. In a reverse process, the juicy berries of the pokeweed bush sometimes appeared reconstituted as purple-flecked scat. Oversized sunflowers seemed drawn by a child's crayon.

October again brought hues that varied in palette according to species and light (both intensity and angle). "Come look!" we often declared to one another. Once more the Knob slowly materialized across the valley as the intervening trees shed their sun-catchers. As an experiment, I stopped cutting whatever it was that had been planted by the landscaper and grew on the northwest slope by the house. What should arise but something wheat-like, reaching seven feet as if herbage on the original Midwestern Prairie. One day I was pushing my grandson on his bicycle when somehow the thing veered into the towering grass. Despite my efforts to discipline the handlebars, the bike plummeted through the brushing and rustling reeds. "Again!"

After a few years on the Estate, we decided to investigate the boulder—relic and monument both. Making our way downhill from the lane and through the woods, we negotiated rough footing, the eye-level branches of scrub pines, the prickles of small hawthorns, and Mr. Licorice, who now seemed like a rivulet of crude oil that trickled over the dead leaves and disappeared. The face of the rock bore dark, delicate leaf-shapes cast by the autumn sun, which was screened by the foliage of a black-gum tree, red and green.

About six feet at its highest and ten at its widest, the rock had side edges that were beveled and slightly pointed. The uphill face was asymmetrical because the top rose a bit on the left. A swale had been carved out at the bottom, probably by rainwater rushing downhill, into, and around the obstacle. This two-foot-deep indentation was roughly outlined by hefty rocks, one of them leaning near the corner from which it had apparently fractured. We descended behind it to view its downhill bulk, its massive rotundity—but instead beheld nothing. Just space behind an upright slab. The top of the rock leaned over the swale almost two feet out of plumb. Its top edge, which we measured as seven inches at its thickest, narrowed to a fairly sharp spine, and the bottom measured only two feet at its widest. How far into the dirt did the rock go? Did it stick into the earth or out of it? To a tentative push the boulder offered no response, nor to a hard one.

Immoveable, yes, but had it flipped out of its stratum after some geological event? Or eroded from its parent-material over the eons? Had a lintel crashed from the Tabernacle of Time? Already moss and lichen were nibbling at it, and a miniature tree had taken root in a crack. Anyway we were the owners, proof being supplied by a stake that was decaying but still orange-flagged.

Did the boulder's front side not trace the line between nature and art? For weren't those long cracks inscriptions? Tell me those aren't two legs that stretch almost parallel to the ground from the body of—why not the fable-furred *Hypax legomenon*?

When Sidney paid a visit, Gigi took him to this grotto. Before she could do anything to prevent him, the almost-four- and-a-half year old planted his left foot on the broken-off fragment, hoisted himself partway up by gripping the boulder's spine, tramped up its face with his sneakers, and straddled it like a horse. "It's easy!" When his Aunt Katie first beheld the slab, up she leaped and folded her torso over the top, head invisible and blue jeans warmed by the declining autumn sun. She finally slid down and leaned against its bright surface. What could a dancer-choreographer do with a rock? "Lots of things," she replied gaily. "You can balance upside down, or on your belly, hip, or knee. You can slide, roll, crawl, lie, melt, press, slam, jump!"

One morning white flakes covered our deck, and neighbors wondered who would first test their all-wheel drives on the steep twists of Annie. Marge declared that snow is her favorite weather—"You can watch it, feel the cold flakes, and see the change in the landscape." You can also hear the wind discharge like a turbine and transform flakes from a dithering jumble to a stream of avengers. Gusts obscured a window or two by whipping up snow-smoke as if from a frozen ground-fire. "Sun," announced Marge cheerily. Snow seemed to be abating under the power of a blue as vivid as the clouds were fast. Patches of the formerly green, bike-swallowing switchgrass (*Panicum virgatum*), were now golden brown, papery stalks that rippled and glowed. White patches on one of "our" horses, which grazed on the steep hill across the highway, reflected the southern rays as if emitting brilliance.

Last year's nest, this year's child.

I happened to wake up around 2:30 a.m. so decided to go outside and view the lunar eclipse, doubly unusual because it was occurring on the winter solstice. I tugged a rag-patch sweater over my pajamas, donned my bathrobe, then wrapped a turtle-neck shirt around my head and neck like the cartoon version of someone with a toothache. Outside I was rewarded by skyrolls of gray insulation. Earthly clouds had blocked the view of the earthly shadow that inched across its satellite. As for the dawn itself—it also turned out to be veiled. All day long the earth's furnace could be imputed only by a feeble lightening of air and a dripping of ice.

Footnote:
1. Richard Connell. *Collier's Weekly*, January 18, 1924

17. Geodyssey VI: "Curve Ahead!"

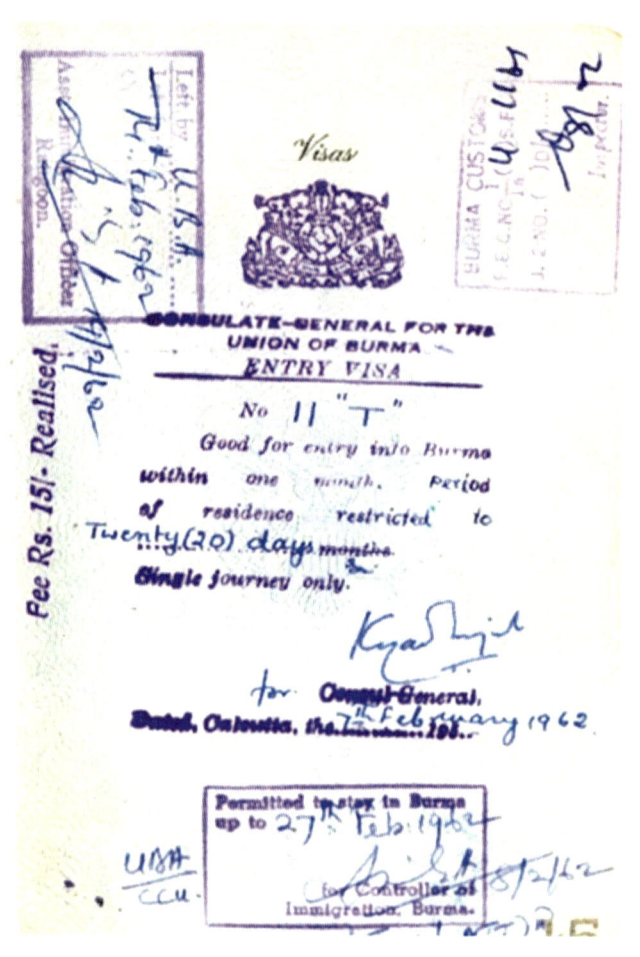

A brightening has reached the floor of the railway-telegraph station and awakened two floor-sleepers. They pack, roll, and lift their gear, then climb down the steps to the wide, quiet, dusty streets of Prome, Burma.

A few days earlier, based at the Salvation Army hostel in Calcutta, we had sought ways of tracing the earth's surface eastward, but the only practical and legal route was by air. So we ended up looking down through pressurized glass at the delta of East Pakistan, a fingered map of itself, and sipping the free beer that made UBA (Union of Burma Airways) popular among youthful travelers.

In Rangoon, the capital of Burma, women in the market wore gauzy blouses and inhaled stogies. Dodge the spit-out betel-blood. Mingle with the throng of brownish Oriental faces. Experience the audible kaleidoscope of unfamiliar consonants, vowels, and pitches. Deal with the usual logistics: finding the YMCA, getting around the lively, decaying city, getting to the hinterland. After a visit to a Buddhist temple, we found a woman guarding our shoes and expecting a tip. Since I was low on currency, I raised my hand and intoned a blessing that caused her to shrink away as if from a curse.

We reached the platform early so as to get dibs on a rack. "Cigarette?" Tom offered the open package in a ritual that had endured throughout Eurasia. "Thanks," I replied, pulling out a Capstan and shouldering the camera in return. At last, from the yards the train slowly rolled in backwards—but what was wrong in this picture? The carriage windows betrayed movement and bundles. We watched in indignation as the train came to a stop, already full of passengers who had carried their stuff down the tracks to the empty cars. So we found ourselves scrambling just to make a nest by the doorway. The carriage budged, and soon its dusky clatter was absorbed and reflected by the jungle-like countryside. Near the open door, Tom leaned back on his rolled-up sleeping bag and dozed while I watched his foot to keep it from extending too far outside.

Several hours later, about midnight, our car was summarily emptied of passengers and onto it climbed a troop of soldiers. We learned that their purpose was to escort the train through unfriendly territory. Having grabbed a couple of seats, we now played dumb and smiled a lot; some man intervened and (bless him) got us permission to stay. When the guns departed around 2 a.m., I inherited a precious baggage rack. After a few hours sleep we reached our station, climbed out, and plopped our bedrolls onto the closest available floor.

Prome, almost 200 miles from Rangoon, seemed a more feasible destination than the half-imaginary Mandalay. So here were, lazing around, cracking jokes in our *dak* bungalow, a wooden structure raised on columns and shaded by trees. It housed chairs that one could lie down in as well as beds furnished with mattresses and mosquito nets. A genial servant would hand us bottles of orange squash. All afternoon we walked, first to a sprawling pagoda that rose crazily from the center of town, then along a sand road enveloped by jungle, where we inhaled flower-scents, pulled off our top shirts, and marveled at the reappearance of forest and shadow in a world of rock and baked mud. A honeymoon without so much as a kiss.

Next day we watched the riverbank recede as our large paddleboat twisted down the Irrawaddy (Ayeyarwady) River toward Rangoon. The balmy air of February clashed with the presence of soldiers, steel shielding, and gun turrets. The lower deck held cargo and the upper deck thirty or so passengers. For two nights we unrolled our mattresses on the hard, barely-swaying surface—the very bags we had wedged between ourselves and the wall of the bunk bed as HMS *Nova Scotia* negotiated the tail of a hurricane. Every few hours the vessel would round a bend and dock gingerly; fruit and merchandise would glide up the ramp balanced on the heads of women. A few times the jungle cleared to reveal a circle of boys who passed a little ball adeptly back and forth with their feet and knees.

February 13 marked my twentieth birthday. To celebrate I joked around with Tom and the man who operated the canteen. He served me French toast (sweetener provided by memory) under Christmas lights strung around a dozen Krishnachrome pictures of elephant gods and many-armed women.

Required to take our second and last airplane, from Rangoon to Bangkok, Thailand, we peered below at wrinkled mountains that were not only forbidding but forbidden. After landing, we stayed at a hotel that offered an extra service to male patrons. In the city, adventures a-plenty but too much sunlight, heat, too many days waiting for my loan to be wired from the States while I had to borrow cash from Tom, MVP of the expedition.

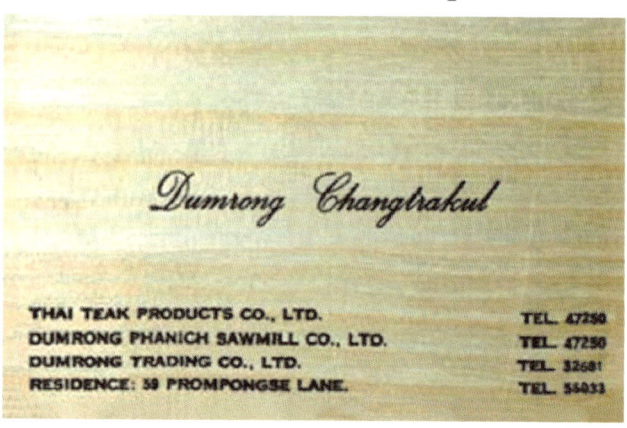

One morning a former teacher at our high school, living in Bangkok on a Fulbright scholarship, lent us an old roofless jeep. Autonomy unfamiliar, exciting, even liberating. Through the countryside we drove it to visit the uncle of my college classmate's. Prosperous and prominent, he regarded us with courteous detachment as we sat near the baby grand. On the way back, alongside rice paddies and sugar-palm groves, we stopped to secure the tailpipe with my rawhide bootlace. As if in a parade, we enjoyed the smiles and waves of people along the road. "No wonder!" laughed our teacher, pointing at Tom, whose pith helmet was fastened under a bushy beard, and at Randy, who wore a red T-shirt with a gaping hole in the back.

Somewhere down the peninsula below Bangkok, I watched in a trance as the rails beneath our observation car screamed off an invisible spool. Standing there under a roof at the end of the train, we bantered with other travelers and shared Tom's smokes. I searched the jungle and groves of rubber for a glimpse of another of those small, conical mountains that glowed pastel in the late afternoon as if sticking out of Planet Malay. Finally the cool wind and the clatter of metal on metal encouraged us take refuge a few yards closer to Singapore.

The next day, ambling along the platform at a stop, I looked up to see cab of our steam locomotive framing the visage of my companion. Down climbed the engineer, who wore a white shirt along with tennis shorts and shoes, and who puffed a cigar as black as he was. "You boys should have come up before!" He continued to remonstrate in a native sing-song that was charmingly at odds with British pronunciation. "You would have met the right person—and would have *learned* something." My boots and hands began negotiating the ladder. Inside, our ebullient host offered us a cigar and warned about the smell. "Is it made of rubber?" I asked, a wisecrack that earned me the driver's seat. As the machine chugged off, I was thrilled at the prospect of immense kinetic power fused with greater control.

Instead I squint through a small, thick, horizontally-oblong pane as if into a periscope at the right flank of a massive black cylinder that wobbles and thrashes along the puny rails, less a mighty guide than a blind monster hurtling full speed while tapping left and right. "*Curve ahead!*" The words barely sound above the intolerable din. Once more those cigar-holding fingers turn various devices that might yet keep the drive wheels from riding the ties or digging a partial grave next to the track—like the engine our Indian train had slowly passed. Terrified, I dare to take another glance at the tracks that seem like a project in Shop class. One of the assistants leans out the left side and yells over the roar, "*Curve up ahead!*" The driver pulls a lever and rotates a wheel, we slow down, and I arise shakily. Tom seems to enjoy his stint as engineer, but all attempts to converse finally cease. At the next station, I repair to my original glide-and-click carriage—learnèd indeed.

After we were able to distinguish the YMCA from the rest of Singapore, I found a copy of *Hamlet* and read it through in a hideaway off an auditorium. All this verbal art—murder and madness in blank verse, revenge miscarried, an imbedded and rhymed playlet, a young man flailing and faking in a sin-stinking world, angels singing him to rest (albeit in the maybe-mood of the subjunctive)—supplied relief from the disordered stimuli of travel. Another balm was salt water. One afternoon we rode a bus with a couple of other vagabonds to the sandy margin of Asia. As we body-surfed in the gleaming waves, I was amazed to be on the opposite side of the same ocean I had waded in as an eight-year-old, after riding down through the snow-walls of Mt. Ranier in my grandfather's Hudson Commodore.

As Tom and I had agreed when we planned the trip, we would now follow divergent itineraries. He wanted to visit Indonesia, where his sister had been an exchange student, and then to Australia; I wanted to see Japan. So our long passport-partnership was over.

At the airport we reminisced about the time our moving vans met up at a toll plaza, and Tom confided that his chauffeur had been awake for more than twenty-four hours: "But he's been snatching some sleep while driving." We recalled a stop on the Pennsylvania Turnpike. Before climbing back into our trucks, I bought a quarter's worth of oxygen from a machine and spasmodically puffed it, whereupon Tom pretended to help me out of the lobby. Surely we recalled climbing the mast of the *Nova Scotia* in the dark as the rigging vibrated noisily. And awakening in a Parisian bus stop next to a *clochard* who pulled up his shirt to reveal a scar from The War. Now at the airport a waitress marched across the carpet and the thuds disoriented me. "Tom—that sound—I thought we were at the White House Hotel!" Located in North Wales, operated by the parents of our shipmate, it had been reached by thumb almost five months earlier.

Our parting is jovial, mellow, and a little beery. I thank him for up-and-volunteering to join me on this expedition and therefore salvaging it. Then I watch as, mustachioed, even tanner after our jaunt to the beach, sporting domed head-armor and trousers cut off into gray walking-shorts, he strides toward the equator.

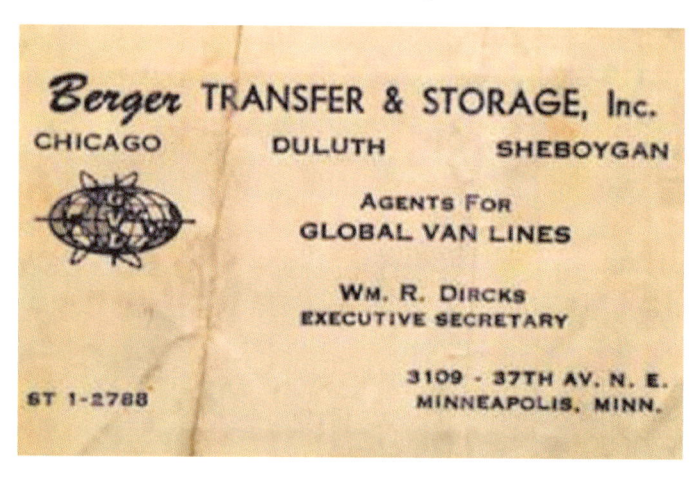

The contract warned, "You know what you're getting into." I signed it, paid $55, and hauled my gear up the ramp to the French ship *Laos*. This name gratified me because this Asian venture had been inspired partly by ferment in the terra incognita of Southeast Asia. My great-toes now squeezed hold of sandals called "thongs," while my boots and winter coat jammed a cheap suitcase along with souvenirs and an Asian edition of my favorite magazine, its cover picturing another earth-circler, John Glenn.

At first a bunch of us young males slept in hammocks that surrounded one of the holds, but partway through the voyage we got transferred to cabins. Mine was Number Douze, which I mistakenly pronounced "Deuxze" and made the steward backtrack from Deux with his cranky key. But the expected comfort turned out to be a little room packed with six men and vented with the same odor that forced us to eat our meals on deck. For the dining room contained about one-hundred caged monkeys, some that had chattered their last, as well as thirty-five crates of eels, some that managed to squiggle onto the floor. In the cabin I watched for one of them to plummet from the vent.

Missing Tom, I wondered what merriment we'd derive from things—like the way the Chinese ate while hunkered atop the picnic-table benches in business suits. I got a kick out of how young people were able to complain in Hebrew, Spanish, English, German, Chinese, Vietnamese, and Indonesian.

Meanwhile, as I learned years afterward, something was touring Tom. He remembers sweating in bed with almost nothing on, while the seventeen-year-old daughter of the family would bring him cool drinks. "I knew I was getting better when I appreciated the daughter more than the ice." (Photo: Tom as Indonesian.)

About our midway port most of the voyagers spoke positively. Saigon, with its classy, old-fashioned buildings, resembled a French provincial city. From a sidewalk table I watched girls pedal by in colorful, flowing outfits, just as they do in heaven. Yet I noticed a few Americans in uniform—a vaguely troubling incongruity like the bombed, burnt-out wing of the palace. Then the ship joined the current of the Mekong River, long and winding, where the serene marshes contrasted ominously with shields on the hull and guards on the deck.

One night as the *Laos* plied the South China Sea toward Hong Kong, I was startled to realize that a constellation had dropped toward the stern.

Japan was cold, gray, and overlong in distance and days even with my host Tsutomu, a former exchange student in high school. With a scrap of paper in hand and eventually a lift from a motorcyclist, I was able to track him down in Tokyo. We hit the rails, on one stop paying a solemn visit to an eerily-new city that had preserved a cement temple to the atom. After we spent the night on the carpet of a ferryboat, which ran from Beppu, the southernmost island, I returned ragged to Kobe and its harbor. Next day I hauled my gear from the YMCA to the *Argentina Maru*, descended far below, climbed to my berth, pulled the curtains, and assumed the fetal position. After four hours I ventured onto the deck into the wind.

"Damn!" From out of the Pacific Ocean jutted a boulder. "How can this be?!" From the rolling surface I beheld even more of these wave-slapped, wandering rocks. Setting my jaw, I thong-padded around and around between stern and bow, motion upon locomotion.

A dozen vignettes for as many days of traveling as the only Caucasian among 724 Japanese who were emigrating to South America:

1. As the weather becomes rough, I return to our bay, its high walls jammed with three-level berths separated by curtains on the front and sides. Behind them infants wail and adults retch and moan. I make a burrow partially with my coat, sewn up this time by Tsutomu's mother. For my personal repair, time is the thread, distance the needle.

2. I hand down an unopened bottle of Dramamine carried from Illinois. The groom, his bride lying beside him, clasps it gratefully and averts his eyes from the box of wedding chocolates he hands up in exchange.

3. The benches and tables of our dining area careen from wall to wall, smashing dishes and nerves. Twice more they are flung around as heavy steel doors break free to slam back and forth. For the next few days, those of us who can eat are served one dish at a time in our dormitory berths. Too alarming to be exciting.

4. The ship now pitches. Again I chat with the man next door, a genial florist from California, and again I draw the curtain and begin reading another escaperback.
5. As the vessel pulls farther from the typhoon, its pitching and rolling decrease. The deck is still off-limits, but I climb the last set of stairs and peer around—just as a wave explodes through round holes in the superstructure.
6. A few of us venture to the dining hall. I have saved $15 by eating native fare on the voyage: lacquered bowls of sticky, tasteless rice, a shred of fish, various little things that seem half animal, half vegetable, noodle-dealies, and egg-chemical soup with spheres that I am pretty sure are not gonads. Yet I enjoy the food, the company, and even the complimentary box of chopsticks with its red-lacquered wood and sliding top.
7. At the canteen, pretzels and beer in hand, or a cup of "cohee," I inspect the map that plots our overnight movement and records our new time. No jet-lag.
8. The days tax and strengthen my patience. Sandals flap against deck to the rhythm of my own whistle, back and forth, around and around, automatically compensating for the rise and fall, never ceasing.
9. Although all clouds have vanished, the blueness of the waves seems deceptive, even sinister against their rolling hill-height. I watch near a bunch of kids as the stern—which towered above the pier in Kobe—dips so far into the trough that the crests of the opposite swells almost reach to the level of the deck. Now up, up, up rises the stern, the sky alone visible and the ship tiny and helpless. Down it plummets as I hold my breath and the rail, and we stare right into the blue mass as it effects a breach over and through the nautical banister, slams down a child, and leaves a swirl of seawater mixed with a little blood.
10. Down in the hold I give another English lesson to the few immigrants to the United States. A hundred of us watch some kind of movie whose reels stretch a few dozen more knots over the Pacific.
11. Kawasaki-san (my neighbor) carries his accordion onto the deck, and at my direction sixty-five junior-high-schoolers sing "My Bonnie Lies Over the Ocean."
12. Up to the left, on the horizon—I am nonplussed to behold a floating object. Low, brown, and horizontal—what is it? A broken-off mass of logs and turf? But isn't that a right angle? These attributes resolved to a pier!

As Kawasaki-san and I walk down the gangplank onto Long Beach, the kids sing "Auld Lang Syne" in Japanese and "My Bonnie" in English. The whole ship resounds with "Goodbye!" The two of us wave and wave, yelling "Sayonara." Scores of arms wave back. "Good-bye, Randy-san!" Out of excitement I have forgotten my bedroll with its microbial travel-decals, but I carry my backpack and suitcase. After up-and-downing over a vast bulge of the globe, I now feel my boot plank-planted.

18. Unfaith Drops In

Ka-klunk! The new boards of the deck darkened with a massive flapping.

From the table I had now and then peered through glass doors that framed the tranquil scene like a photograph in a calendar. Across the valley two white eggs, taller than the house near them, stood parallel to the deck-rail. These Bradford petals glowed around the edges and then turned dull every time a morning cloud-shadow raced across them and up the pasture while peeling the dark grass to bright green.

Now a hang-glider must have crashed onto the café atop the Chartreuse Range! But this was Virginia: had a large animal fallen off the roof? I shot from the chair and discerned a pair of—what were they? Outsized wings! And did they not attach to a human shape?

As it labored to arise, I slid open one door and screen, rushed out and, as the figure lifted its head, beheld the dazed face of a woman.

"Thanks," she said weakly. "Guess I misjudged."

I reached under her arms and strained to help her get up. She tucked her legs, covered with insulated pants that extended to boots, under a white robe. As she squeezed her wings through the doorway, they sprang open a bit and one fanned an orchid on the table.

"Be careful! My wife counts the flowers on that stalk." I helped her settle in a dining room chair and brought her a glass of water. After a few moments I asked if she could tell me who she was.

"I am Unfaith, the Angel of Unbelief."

Straight gaze, no wink. I was embarrassed to recall an ad in the window of Victoria's Secret: "Even angels need a little lift."

What did *I* need? A witness. Months earlier I had beheld a white rainbow that spanned the back acres, so into the house I ran to pull Marjory out for a look. But now I imagined this exchange: "There are only twelve blooms on my orchid!" "Honey, it was the Angel of Unbelief."

After staring at this—arrival, I introduced myself.

"Yes," she replied matter-of-factly. "What?" again—did she know me? And again I regarded her, dumbfounded. This angel, I slowly perceived that she was not the—well, the Regulation Caucasian. Her skin mixed light brown and daffodil. And instead of long, curly locks she had a spiky do, her arms were muscular rather than willowy, and a few pounds less might have gotten her over the railing. Satan's sister is kicked out, crashes onto my deck, and has something on me. I stole a glance through the side window but realized that my wife had only begun her church service.

"Can you tell me," I asked falteringly, "why you came here?"

"Randall, I heard your prayer!"

"My—?" I couldn't even remember how to clasp my hands in supplication, although sometimes I knelt at the bed to look for slippers.

"For encouragement."

I shook my head as memory rewound to an hour earlier. I had been reading the newspaper, which reported the new president's words: "And people of no faith." Dramatically inclusive, they followed his inaugural recognition of "non-believers." I had thought, "We finally get some major respect." Yet despite the new season of the year and my new first-class citizenship, the old uneasiness returned. Looking up from the newspaper I had gazed at the nascent foliage—yellow-green on the tulip poplars and rust on the red maples, ironic for new growth. I already struggled to deal with no assurance that life has meaning or purpose, with no sense of otherworldly guidance or comfort, with no hope of a better life beyond this one, with no benefit of shared faith. But to be an oddball in a world of devotees…. I remembered wishing fervently for another boost.

"You have a nice place. With thick logs." To my relief she sounded less shaken, and she now inspected the vaulted ceiling of pine. "Knotty constellations."

"Uh-huh." Around her eyes the impressions left by the goggles had filled in. I remembered how two-year-old Sidney had discovered a pair by the swimming pool, wrestled them on with my help, and peered out uncertainly from their grip.

When her glance fell upon a nearby wine bottle, I wondered if possibly—would she like something other than water? Soon the corkscrew had done its job. Then I cast about for a topic. "Unfaith," I offered, "my friend Richard said that we agnostics and atheists are the last ones in the closet."

"Indeed. We're not only *not* out, we're *with*out, supposedly. We're *ag*-nostics—or rather *a*-gnostics—so we don't *know*. Or we're *a*-theists, without a deity." She gave her glass a red swirl. "We're faith-less, god-less, even in-fidels. Kafirs. We're not 'spiritual,' so I guess we're soul-less, just materialistic. A collection of atoms."

"A collection, yes, but not just."

"In fact don't you think human beings make the miraculous superfluous? To conceive of symbols! To speak, listen, write, read, paint, sing, even think, all more wondrous than to stroll on waves. Randall, even the ability to imagine the supernatural itself. Yet unless we think of ourselves as divinely-sparked, we're accused of being—mechanical."

"Wind me up, Scotty!" I watched in vain for a smile. She took another sip and folded her arms, unlike angels elsewhere that hold their hands in prayer or rest them on their knees demurely. To keep things going, I asked what she liked to be called.

"Unfaith."

"I mean, like 'secular humanist,' or 'freethinker'…."

"Hmmm.... Isn't that last one impossible?" At my puzzled look she went on. "Well, in order to think, one has to manipulate concepts, which depend on language and culture, which already organize life in an arbitrary way."

"OK," I thought, "a feathered professor." And replied, "So true."

"That word 'spiritual,' for example. There's no equivalent that's otherworldly-free. No word to express awe at the universe, love for family and friends, concern for humans and other beings, appreciation of the earth and its...."

I held a remembered hardball: fingering its sphere-and-stitches, I threw it—first sensing the increasing weight, then the sudden independence. This example of physical pleasure—maybe inappropriate, so I tried another. "Unfaith, you won't forget creativity. I mean as a product and a process, too."

"Ah, yes, 'Sealed in the amber of art.' " Her fingertips made aerial quotation marks. "I notice the collection on your walls." Would she ask who had photographed the rural people of Haute-Loire? No, she continued to ruminate. "There's a paradox here because so much art is influenced by religion." She threw out an unfamiliar name.

"Who's Andy Freud?"

"An...die...*Freude*," she repeated as if I had to read her lips. "Schiller's poem, Beethoven's song. Joy springs ultimately from God, but—"

"I'm sure you're right. 'About Freedom.'"

Was she smiling behind the glass rim? "Well, I suppose it can be translated that way. That word 'free'—Randall, we distrust it." My glass stopped in midair. "Everybody thinks it's a desideratum, so they harmonize whatever-beliefs with it. Do you follow me? Every dogma must be liberating—if only from fear or aimlessness, even from freedom itself."

I struggled to keep up: "Somebody said 'Freedom is perfect control.'"

"Yes, but control of oneself by oneself, or by something else?" Now what should she do but burst into song: "Perfect submis-sion, all is at re-est." My eyes stuck open as I took one or two sips toward composure before asking what she believed.

"Nothing is holy, much is precious."

This proclamation echoed from the walls, floor, and ceiling. Out of the knotholes seemed to spring branches, needles, cones, even a whiff of pollen. "Oh," I heard myself say, repressing a sneeze. After a few long moments I gave myself a refill and, when she regarded her empty glass, did the same for my visitor.

"Randall," she declared gravely, "the basis of religion is not reason. It's like art in that respect, don't you think? It arises from a mode of apprehension other than the empirical. For example, if somebody came to earth from outer space—"

"Like somebody I know," I murmured.

"—how likely would they be to imagine a benevolent power-in-charge? Or an array of them? Oh, look at those goldfinches!" The pair on the deck-rail seemed entrusted with the world's standard of yellow.

"They're like a blessing from on high," I said, "if there were such a thing."

"Randall, there's a holy bestiary—wholly irrational if you allow my word-play. Among religions past and present. A tortoise that carries the world like a backpack, jaguars, lynxes, sphinxes.... The Bible is itself an ark that carries a talking serpent, the Lion of Judah, an entire deck of sheep, the Beast by Land and Sea—"

"Dominick the Donkey." This wisecrack drew that nobody-home expression.

"Doves, of course," she continued, "that must be sacrificed to Jehovah for various infractions. Maybe a pigeon for extra credit."

Why couldn't I get a sweet angel like the one on the shelf of the Trading Post next to Death riding a Motorcycle? I remembered her delicate lips and décolleté prom dress. "Yes, a sacred zoo." Fighting an impulse to check the clock, I reflected for a moment. "At least there's no throwing children down a well in Yucatan," I asserted, "or freeze-drying them on some peak of the Andes—"

"But child sacrifice may be closer than you think. In war, many a 'supreme sacrifice' has been made for our deity against theirs."

"So God himself" I thought, "can be drafted." Uneasily I wondered about holy murder. Was it not basic to the creed I had forsaken? As if in a vision, I sat in Bible school again while a projector clicked out black-and-white images. Another boy labored up a mountain with a donkey piled with brush, whereupon his father tied him down on an altar, lifted a knife—and ceased at the command of an angel. I recalled our Isaac who failed to escape the olive-timbers and iron.

"—like that word 'faith.'" She had been continuing her lecture in my absence. "We try to avoid it."

"But how?"

"We prefer 'belief.' It's a neutral term, so it has to operate without a subsidy. If I might refer to our catechism. 'What is faith?'" Again she poked the air. "'Faith is belief wearing a surplice.' Randall, we even distrust belief since it can give rise to certainties that are at best fanciful and at worst destructive." I remembered a guy in Pakistan who assured me that Christ hadn't risen from the dead because his underclothes were preserved in Kashmir.

"So you *believe* that belief is untrustworthy."

"Conundrum granted. But we try to anchor our ideas in observation, evidence, logic, capacity for amendment. To humans, reason is a servant they don't mind grabbing by the ear. They crave order, or a sense of it, to combat the unruliness of life. Take cause-and-effect relationships—people will readily invent them. Especially the operation of sacred powers. Maybe we should dribble some of this wine onto the ground"—she tipped her glass a bit over the flooring—"to appease the gods. They would appreciate the hint of oak."

Trying to keep up, I ventured a bon mot of my own: "Unfaith, do you know why you don't run across Superman on your flights?" She shook her head. "Because phone booths are obsolete."

She stared before resuming in earnest. "We're skeptical of so-called divine intervention, higher powers—well-meaning or hostile. Notions passed down by tongue or text."

"And holy scriptures?"

"According to our Right Wing (I don't mean to be severe), they are merely haphazard scrapbooks bound by ethnicity and era. But my group is more—more latitudinarian. We imagine various scriptures as an attic—voluminous, dim, invitingly jumbled. Under a bare light bulb, see how the obsolete leans against the seasonal, how the useless and workaday jam a trunk along with the...."

"Attic!" I thought as she continued her picture of a thousand words. *That's* where I put those Akkadian fragments!"

She continued. "Yet under an ice skate or a tilted birdcage," she went on, "behold a gleam of treasure—"

"Such as?"

"The parables of Jesus. Some of these are Hope Diamonds of humanism. But all the scriptures of major religions were written before the insights of geology, genetics, astronomy, anthropology, sociology, sociobiology, psychology, paleozoology, astrobiology—"

"Orthodontics."

She betrayed a smile and continued. "We're even more skeptical about the word 'know,' which often means 'believe.' As you may recall from Philosophy 101, anything that is *known* must be *true*. Yet by definition theology cannot be established as fact."

"Unfaith, I used to tell my students that there's too much knowing in life, so don't be afraid to say 'Beats me.'"

"Babashanda!" She held out her glass for a toast. "Most of us skeptics, we're not like religious fundamentalists of any stripe—we're inclined to tolerate uncertainty and ambiguity, and some of us even enjoy them. We like to reflect upon instead of just reflect." I started to warm toward this character even though she had violated Ann Landers' injunction never to drop in.

"That kind of belief—can you give me an example?"

"Bearded theology."

"Did you say 'bearded'?"

"Yes, patriarchal. The Men Upstairs." I was taking in her idea with a couple of sips when a phrase came into my head—"Old and New Testicles"—and politely stayed there.

"Believers will do anything to keep deities as fact. Randall, do you know what Jean de la Fontaine wrote?"

"M-mmm."

"'Everyone believes very easily whatever he fears or desires.'"

I supposed that "everyone" included me but asked, "How can people be so hard-boiled about practical matters and then be so—I mean how can they not—"

"Not notice the bar-code on Santa's gift? What would be their motivation?" Silence. In a kindly tone she asked, "Would you want all people to be like you? To disown a cosmology that secures them to life like gravity?" I remembered Alzbeta, who had enlisted the husky: in her Slavic accent she had fervently declared that God had helped her not only during The War but afterward when she suffered from dangerous effects.

"I guess not."

"Randall...." She paused. "Do you think that some people are born to believe?" I imagined these last three words as a tattoo. Then I remembered Ernest Lion. Once while holding open a screen door to welcome me, he exposed the numbers engraved on his forearm arm, the 9s plumply European. After his experience in concentration camps he had lost his faith—until his last days when he converted to Roman Catholicism and declared, "A person has to believe in something."

I heard my name. "Sorry, Unfaith, just thinking. Anyway, belief doesn't necessarily make you a robot. One of my colleagues was a devout Catholic, but he was also a scholar of an eminent Protestant— somebody he venerated enough to give their child the middle name Tyndale."

Again that rich alto voice: "By the light of bur-ning mar-tyrs." These stray and enigmatic lyrics accompanied her examination of the orchid. I watched her eyes as they began with the leaves—which rippled horizontally away from the pot, glossy and turgid—then followed the stem upward to where it became a T, and finally traced one group of petals with their fine, light-purple veins.

"Unfaith, doesn't each group of petals—one-two-three-four-five—look like a pinwheel?"

"Yes. Or like a prayer-wheel." After a moment she lifted her gaze to the chain-suspended lamp. "Oh, they're convex! A merry-go-'round of fruits! Which is your favorite?"

"Hmm." I looked at my wine glass: "The grape!" At this she beamed, and again we made our crystal ring out like—like—

"God's doorbell!" she exclaimed merrily. She held out her glass and began making slow back-and-forth dips with it as she sang to the familiar tune: "Amaa-zing grapes, how sweet the sound/ Of corks being pulled out fre-ee,/ I o-once was dry, but then I downed/ Your white and burr-gundy." She stopped abruptly: "I think it's an instinct."

I could only stammer, "What is?"

"Faith. Belief. Not so much a matter of temperament but of survival—over millennia. Prevenient wiring." She pursed her lips and stared at the table. "So ironically, Randall, that would make faith a necessary condition for your own skepticism."

"Excuse me?"

"Well, it probably helped people to survive and become your forebears." A story flashed to mind: Sophia, a Christian Scientist, became furious when she discovered that a lodger was making beer in her cellar during The War. "Randall, they survived disease, famine, war, heartbreak, and whatever, thanks to confidence in ultimate meaning—and to the stick-together that people get from religion."

"So my spiritual ancestors enabled me to exist and to doubt."

"Yes," she chuckled; "they created a *Nonster*."

I cast about for a change of subject. "Unfaith, may I by any chance ask what your—your synod enjoys with wine, you know what kind of food?"

A serious gaze: "Pasta angelicus." She laughed gaily.

This direction unpromising, I tacked. "Well, let me ask: why are angels usually female?"

"This gender business…." She continued with a hint of weariness. "The psalm says that God shall cover thee with his pinions, and his angels used to be males, but they seem to have become feminized. Ancillary in the Latin sense, you know, as handmaidens."

I truly knew that I didn't want to correct an imbalance. What if she intended to recruit me! Could I get a postponement this time, too? I vowed that Clarence's bell would not jingle up a new set of wings.

The grape now eased another change of subjects. "Unfaith, I don't understand how people can be so certain about 'God,'" remembering to punctuate with my fingers. "My friend Tom says there's more evidence for the existence of the Easter Bunny: 'I've seen the eggs.'"

"Let me share a bit more of our catechism." She assumed a formal tone: 'Is there a god?' 'It matters not.'" These words froze airborn and hung like icicles—as in the tale of Paul Bunyon. I started to object but she interrupted. "Such a venerable has little interest in its own creation. 'No deity on duty,' we say."

I let the maxim sink in. "In other words—"

"Suppose a divinity of some type created the world—even the universe. This can be a harsh and precarious existence, yet do people really get help from 'above'?" (Fingers flicked.) Still, humans tend to count on religions for what we call HELP—Heavenly External Locus of Power. It can be the source of meaning and even goodness. So this is one way that earthlings can deal with life."

"And another way?"

"To conclude that the notion of an all-powerful and benevolent god is mocked by this rolling palimpsest of misery."

I caught the idea, give or take a few syllables. About a minute passed as she shuffled wings and we tipped crystal. "Unfaith, as for the eternal—there's a big rock on our property that's older than God!" At her quizzical look, I explained: "It's older than humans, so it stood there before their godly conceptions."

She nodded: "Rock of Ages."

"But I wonder—don't you admit that believers can be right, theoretically? That the devout actually hear God's voice? And that we ourselves should listen?" I thought for a moment. "Or perhaps HELP is a kind of radio station that only some people can receive."

"We acknowledge, respect, and even venerate the unknowable."

Again she assumed a formal intonation: "'What is mystery?' 'Mystery lives at the pleasure of humility.' And Randall, the very day you can prove a negative, you can square a circle or make a note on a piano grow louder. Holy communion, for example." She held something invisible aloft between thumb and finger. "Wafer Miraculous or Wonder Bread? And can anyone prove that there is or is not a heaven?"

"Well," I declared ruefully, "I bet that more people in the United States believe in angels than in evolution." Several feathers rippled. She turned to gaze at birds that stood on the ground pecking at knocked-over seeds. "Sorry, Unfaith, what I mean is, they can't even adapt their theology to an axiom of science."

"Please go on," she said without warmth.

"I was channel-surfing one day and there was this guy who said a bird was spotted in Indonesia that resembled a pterodactyl so it must be one. I guess this showed that all animals were created at the same time. The narrator spoke with such bland conviction—I had to wonder if it was Jonathan Winters puttin' me on."

A wasted reference to the comedian, but Unfaith did seem to mull over my grievance. "Piety," she declared, "drives slow in the intellectual fast lane. You can understand how believers can feel threatened. Who wants a continuum that runs back from human beings to earlier versions and then to ever more primitive forms?"

"Adam the African?"

Grinning at my revision of Genesis, she continued. "Several religions teach that human beings were uniquely created in God's image. And for most Christians—to raise the stakes—one of these humans is also God. He can't be a long-tressed, ethereal descendant of an all-over hairy hominin. So zoological evolution tosses a fossil through the stained glass."

With a touch of ceremony I poured us a refill and then pursued a tangent. "I saw a TV documentary on giant prehistoric birds that killed early humans. There was this scene where a pair of young women tried to run away from a beak swooping down behind them—then you heard a 'Whump!' and only one escaped."

Unfaith sniffed her wine. "At least Jupiter-swan created a life." Shutting her eyes, she recited these syllables: "'Lapsèd here below,/E'en wings waft woe.'"

My guest seemed to await a response. "The poet," I offered.

"Yes, Salvia Divinorum. My translation. Something to do besides watch out for hawks and hunters."

Did she plan to have company out there? I felt a tremble of dread, but at least I would never walk alone. Or fly. "Mm-hm."

Unfaith zoned out for a while and then picked up an earlier thread of conversation. "Randall, you'll invite needless anxiety if you think of believers as a monolith. Even the followers of Jesus—"

"It's always been like trying to herd Catholics. I knew this Methodist who declared that Jesus was a space traveler who zoomed from world to world. I even knew another bright fellow, partly Native American—he followed the Book of Common Prayer but he seemed to feel the divine most keenly in nature."

"An Episco-pantheist! Lots of non-conformity. And aren't many of the faithful *faders*—in and out like a short-wave signal. 'What is doubt?' 'Doubt is the stalk of the sunflower of faith.' Randall, do you think there could actually be more disparity among believers than between believers and unbelievers?"

I rattled the idea around my baldness. "Good question to enjoy never being able to answer."

Through the screen came a distant barking that was carried off by the breeze. "Schisms, heresies…." With her left hand she rubbed the skin near her eyes where the goggles had pressed. Up went the fingers. "'Winch theological slack,/Loosen bones on the rack.'"

Silence. "Righteous violence—another reason why people distrust religion. Also plenty of conflict that hurts without a scream. Even within congregations. This church we attended, it had this gorgeous stained glass 'way above the altar. The window is still in one piece—or twelve, a triangle for each apostle—but the congregation is fractured. The man who donated the object never sees it." In a non-spiritual postscript, I thought, "Lotta bucks."

"There are rifts among us, too. The Right-Wingers favor confrontation, but we urge humility, goodwill, even respect. Some of us nonbelievers feel sympathy and even affection toward religion, although some hiss at it."

"Well," I declared, rustling the newspaper, "I invite anyone to read about yesterday's world and try to defend the idea of a just deity. And I roll my eyes at the idea that we need a king, lord, prince…."

"Ironically, this class of personages is itself—well, made up."

"Unfaith, yes, it's a sort of caste, I think.

Fingers in air: "'Where does royalty live?' 'In Fallacy Palace.'"

On I went. "Father, master—even a shepherd! *B-a-a*. Anyway, I would never plead with some benevolent authority figure to—you know, do the job."

"You mean prayer of petition." I nodded. "We call it 'Please-on-the-knees.'"

"Ring-kissing. Not for myself, not for my country, not for my grandson."

"But 'When sorrows like sea-billows roll'?" At this sibilant prospect I tried to blank out. "Prayer can be a vital comfort," she went on. "And how selfless to pray for others! But when we might instead try to shoulder a burden, or lighten it, we can stay passive by asking for help, even avoid responsibility. You know the proverb: 'Dona dona *no*bis, makes a person *o*bese.'"

I searched my memory but just smiled as we toasted again. Peering over crystal, I wondered if her cheeks had a sprinkling of freckles. Then I found myself circling back. "If I did kneel and put my hands together, I wouldn't conclude with 'If it be thy will.' Why ask somebody to do something and then say 'If you want to'?"

She choked briefly on a sip. "Maybe we can go back to the question of skepticism. How can some people, despite the forces of instinct and social—"

"Unfaith, some unbelievers have had disagreeable experiences. I knew this fellow who used to honk every time he drove past a school where nuns packed rulers. Something that still galls me: when our friend was divorced after two children and almost two decades, she got a notice of annulment addressed to her maiden name. She was weeping when we happened to arrive. Friend Tom told a story about his grandparents, who went to the World's Fair in Chicago in 1893. They were criticized for being too worldly, partly because Little Egypt danced on the midway. The church did not regard the fair as educational for teachers. So they were shunned and lost their jobs. His father always suspected another cause: "Grandpa had ordered building supplies from Sears and the local hardware store owner wanted to punish them.""

"If true, worldly for sure."

"As for other doubters, Unfaith…. You know the old saying, 'God never gives us too heavy a load'—well maybe he did."

"The divine divvier of burdens." After a moment: "Another reason for skepticism—the acts of some apostles."

"Oh—look at the way soldiers from West Pakistan treated their Muslim sisters in East Pakistan when it seceded." I felt my teeth clench. Then I jumped from violent to dubious. "How about way people indoctrinate their kids. 'Mommy, what do we believe?' Once our daughter came back from a church daycare and asked, 'Why does Jesus make the sun come out and sweat us?' Her own four-year-old recently committed heresy: 'Hi Grandpa, my elephant died to heaven last night but came back because he didn't like God.' But the lad became more orthodox after a few months: 'You go to heaven'—almost cheerful —'Hey, God! And you start living again!' The way children are molded—it reminds me of the way country boys were sewn into long underwear for the winter." She tilted her head as if trying to hear me. "In old-time South Carolina, out in the country."

"Ironically, Randall, doctrine is a function of latitude and longitude. *Where* you are is *what* you are."

"No Mormons among Muslims." The alliteration pleased me.

With a twinkle: "Not much Voodoo on the Volga."

I pressed the subject: "And along with this geographical grid, there's a socioeconomic one, no?" Angling for respect: "It's all so—so deterministic."

"Yes, accidentals become essentials." One-upped again. "By the way," she continued, "did you know that every challenge that we make to religion has already been tackled by theologians? And many freethinkers are interested in theology. Have you ever read *The Five Gospels* by the Jesus Seminar and—"

"Nope."

"How about *Jesus, Interrupted* by Ehrman?" "Uh-uh. But I have read *Angels & Demons*."

"Kitsch."

"No, Brown—Dan Brown."

Her glass stopped momentarily before she took a final swallow and mused for a while. As we sat, feathers scuffed and clicked a bit the floor. "Nice Swiffers," I thought. I recalled congregants whose best qualities seemed reinforced by devotion. And the services—those communal-spiritual restoratives. And the missionaries who had welcomed me to Asia, sheltered and healed me from it. I also pictured my wife as she asked the blessing as she herself graced the table. "It would be a brave person," I asserted, "who could dismiss religion entirely. I would never say that it has no merit—"

"Unlike astrology," she replied. "Nonsense divided into twelve parts. A fancy pan with no pizza. A spandrel supreme."

I nodded wisely. After a companionable silence I declared: "Of course logic isn't the most important thing."

"Said the snowman as he wound his scarf tighter."

Not sure how to take this rejoinder, I said, "Unfaith, you are a whiz at the epitaphs." This compliment drew a slightly quizzical frown. "Epigraphs." After another silence, I tried again: "Epi—"

"Grams?"

Again reduced to a nod, I changed course. "Does your group have any policy about living in a world of faith?"

"Yes. Never challenge people gratuitously. Because they could be right, or partly right. Besides, their values and yours could overlap enough that there's little practical concern.

And they might even be better than you. Also their feelings could be hurt and their beliefs won't change anyway, so they might…."

"Resent the snot out of you."

"More accurate than eloquent, dear host. But in the public marketplace, believers should not expect to tender holy scrip. Civic religiosity is—well, wings on a horse."

"Hmm. Like the Pledge of Allegiance—I just cough at 'under God.'"

"You'll notice that this phrase contradicts 'with liberty' because the Pledge forces *Nons* to honor some kind of vague established religion."

She mulled over the idea for a while. "A faithful citizen in two senses—fused and mutually reinforcing. And a ceremonial monarch, strangely enough, crowned by a democracy." She pondered the subject. "But it probably goes against DNA not to harmonize the religious and political. Yes, the Constitution does forbid a religious establishment, but that goal may be—I'll call it 'desirably unnatural.'"

"Official disestablishment, anyway. I think that for many people the stripes of the flag were dyed in the blood of the lamb. Born-agains even got us an elected-again president."

"Randall…. " She considered for a few moments. "I wonder if you would be happier in a country like England. Or France—it's 'post-Christian,' although the mosques are full of men's shoes."

"Well, I did enjoy living there without seeing a fish on a car."

"Why would anybody—"

"Not important.

If I lived in Europe, though, what about my grandson? Who would make the boy laugh by putting himself into Time Out?"

"Bad Grandpa," she grinned. "Going back to a deity-democracy.

'When do you bring in God?'" she intoned. "'When you've run out of ideas.'"

"Catechism." She nodded.

The pessimistic part of my arm sensed that the glass was half empty. I offered to refill hers, too, but she covered it with a hand: "Flying." In a while she looked at me with concern. "Randall, about living in the rural South—other areas owe less fealty to Jesus."

"Do you know why they call him 'the Lord'?" She shook her head. "'The Duke' has already been taken." Not the moment to introduce John Wayne, so I picked up on geography. "What about hell—to some citizens of this region, it's more popular than the beach."

"Your thoughts, please?"

"OK. The universe comes into existence billions of years ago, then eventually a speck materializes, which circles a star for a few billion more while animals begin eating each other alive. This new species develops by trial and error, and if they're not chewed up and swallowed, they experience a more sophisticated variety of pain. Do you know the story of Rapunzel?"

"Ra—Not a name I recognize."

"She was stuck away atop a fancy tower, where she sang—"

"Tower!? Randall! Did she have incredibly long, orange hair?" I nodded and kept my mouth from falling open. "That was one of our landmarks! She used to sing in a dialect—German? Czech? Perhaps a blend. She'd notice us and sing: 'Could I but fly with thee…. Could thy white feathers cool my streaming-backward flames….' Or maybe 'backward- blazing'…. Or—"

"Please stop!" I wanted to yell.

"Or whatever. Next time I flew past, the tower looked empty."

Photo by author

"Stop!" I thought. "Will Mrs. McGregor come to the door with a warm pie?!" Dizzy, I had to get back to the real world. "Anyway, Unfaith, this species I was talking about, humans, they learn that their sins are *everything*. In fact the main concern of the God of Galaxies. Luckily he'll withhold punishment, an eternal kind, no less—as long as they believe that he sacrificed himself, you know, as propitiation."

Silence. "Randall, we call that alternative 'Believe or burn.' It's an either-or premise, in this case a fallacious and anti-intellectual one. I would even have to call it logophobic."

I would, too, no doubt, but shifted to an anecdote. "One of my students gave a speech persuading us that hell is a topic to be reckoned with in the New Testament. She showed around an open Bible that was liberally underlined—in red, no less. Point proven.'"

"Christian brimstone…. Koranic boil-or-roast." She looked a bit stricken. "Unimaginable imaginary cruelty. Not enough of it here. And you can't escape there." She stood with some commotion and raised her arms with palms upward: "'Folks like you and me/Beg for Zyklon B." Sitting again, carefully, she leaned her head back and watched a cloud float safely across the wood-framed Bermuda Triangle of sky. Then she pursed her lips and blew gently on the orchid as it to make it twirl. After a lull she asked, "Randall, who is the man in the photograph, the one looking out—is that a window?"

"A hole cut into the logs. That's my late brother—he died soon after that." Her gaze turned quickly to me: "You have my sympathy. Were you close?"

I didn't try to speak. Then I pointed across the treetops: "Do you see that little shack in the middle of the field?"

She rose halfway up and studied the shallow valley. "Leaning a bit, with a rusty roof."

"On this side of it in the shade—there's a mound. One day my brother handed me our binoculars and urged me to take a look, and I made out junk in the form of an old sedan." The memory doubtless caused me to look a bit taken aback, for she reached over and laid her warm hand on my arm for a second. I slapped the newspaper with my other hand. "Here's the Reverend Billy Graham, he's answering a letter from somebody who's drifting. 'God has a plan for your life—so why not seek it?' Unfaith, I myself could do better than God!"

"Please don't get wrought up," she urged gently.

"Here's an example. When our grandson was a couple of years old, he got sick on a visit. We comforted him right there on the couch where I once shed tears for my brother. I encouraged him to take his medicine—swallowed a pretend-dose of it, yum yum! Now here's my plan: I would have given that illness to my brother instead so he wouldn't go on a strenuous bike-ride—and when he got well he could have met my grandson."

Silence. "Randall, you look distrait."

I surveyed the field with its installation surrounded by a half-circle of weeds left by the tractor. "Sometimes I imagine that when a bit of chrome gleams, you know, remnant of a bumper, he's signaling me mischievously, or that when nobody comes to the shack's drive-in window, we lay on the horn, or that when we drive around the field at night, we shift gears, bounce, and laugh."

"A memorial shed."

I peered down the long driveway but knew that Sunday school had just begun. "Unfaith, there's something I call the *Shenandoah* principle. Ever see that movie?" Again she shook her head as I belatedly watched her squeeze down a row of popcorn boxes. "This family hopes to ride out the Civil War in isolation here in Virginia, on a farm, but most of them get killed. One woman is raped, murdered, and thrown down a well. It's O.K. because Junior comes limping home on his crutch just at church time, and everybody sings the Doxology."

"'From God all blessings flow,'" she recited; "'but whence the stubbèd toe?'"

Before she could name the poet, I ran on. "Believers look at a mountain and see God's power. But the Chartreuse Range in France—there's a famous monastery tucked inside it—during the Middle Ages part of that upthrust ocean floor tumbled onto a village."

Her face turned solemn. "*Avalanche*—un mot français. Swallowed up."

Into a dimly-lit room of memory came a wan girl, suffering from tuberculosis, who led a water buffalo over the dirt floor as Tom and I ate curry with her parents. "We're playthings to forces inside the earth, atop it, and even outside it. Even to invisible bits of deadly life—it's not just the boll weevil that's lookin' for a home." I quickly abandoned pop songs. "If that's not enough, we're vulnerable to each other." What I really thought was that human beings, like birds on The Estate, shit in their own water.

My guest stayed motionless for a while. "Like the old saying, 'Careless, Callous, and Cruel/Travel by limo and mule.'" Or by pickup truck, as I suddenly remembered. One late afternoon around Halloween, as I walked to my trailer in Connecticut, an arm reached out the oncoming rolled-down window and lobbed something at me. I twisted quickly enough to deflect it from my descendants—but onto my date. Bent and splattered with Humpty Pumpkin, she managed to say "It hurts" before asking if I was O.K. I now wondered about the two young guys, jerks, if they would become their own victims to one extent or another. If they would bring pulp and pain into their own lives.

"People can even die of themselves."

At my proclamation she made a brief frown. "Yes, individually and collectively. Secular humanists are sometimes accused of vapid optimism, Randall. I don't guess you'd fit that description."

"No Easter without Lent."

Again her brow furrowed. "I admire that philosophy. May I ask the source?"

"A minister, our friend."

She laid her chin in a hand. "You mentioned sin. Could we talk about it?"

"Hit me with your rhythm stick."

"Beg your pardon?"

"Please go ahead."

"To be one of us *Nons* you don't have to be a wretch. You may *be* one, or *feel* like one, but you don't have to drone on about it in the pentatonic scale."

I had little in common with the Pentecostals, so these words zipped over my head. I checked my glass, took a final sip, and declared, "We'll run out of oil in this world long before we run out of sin."

"It will never fall into desuetude."

"Christianity runs on it. 'Feed me, Seymour!'" Quickly I tried another phrase: "No sin, no savior. So they may even perceive evil where it doesn't exist."

"And of course ignore the possibility of it when convenient. But it costs people not to feel they know, so they don't mind fashioning their own truth."

"Costs?" I repeated.

"Yes, uncertainty can be liberating, but—let me give you an extreme example. Once a fog came up and I lost my sense of direction, my speed, height, angle of pitch and roll. I had no boundaries, just cool, humid whiteness to soar around in. But I was terrified because there was no fixed point of reference. I decided to flap slower and descend enough to catch a glimpse of something yet still clear the wires. Nonetheless I could have rammed into anything high, a building, a tower, a hill—"

"Or a steeple."

Her face tightened. "Then a dark blur materialized under me, which I figured was a narrow asphalt road. But as I tried to follow it, the pavement seemed to recede behind me much too fast for the effort I was making to fly. I dropped lower, only to hear a continuous rumbling racket. Then the road became this black slurry, which I made out to be segmented, contrary to the laws of physics. Just before I lost my wits, what should I recognize but mounds of coal headed the opposite way. The noise suddenly abated and I beheld a pair of steel lifelines."

My eyes were wide open. "Unfaith, I'm so glad you survived!" I felt sheepish about wishing that she resembled the angel at the Trading Post who wore a white porcelain gown so thin and clinging as to merge with her thigh. "What did you do next?"

"Followed the tracks slowly, always trying to stay above any sudden headlight, always on guard not to be brained at a crossover. Then a viaduct loomed up, and just in time I slowed enough to climb far enough to alight on its railing. There I waited for the mist to rise."

The clock ticked silently. "Unfaith, does that mist not resemble the universe?"

She seemed to look at a knothole for a moment. "In space there is no east or west."

"No up or down, no in or out." I took in the valley-view, now bright in the noonday sun. "From up here on the ridge I've looked down onto a bowl of whipped cream, and I've seen fog so thick you would never even guess there was a world. But this ghostly foliage materialized nearby, maybe the silhouette of a branch, maybe one that ends as a bird-shape. Then more vegetation, and finally the roofs of the village—like Brigadoon."

"What kind of dune?"

"No, d-o-o-n, it's the name of a village in Scotland. It's a magical one that reappears every hundred years."

Did I detect a frown? "We're not keen on magic," she replied. "Something freethinkers can live without."

"Sister Soberwings!" I teased. "I can guess what you think about the place known as heaven."

"How do you feel about it, Randall."

"Hmmm…. " I searched for a response.

"Lanyards."

"Excuse me?"

"We used to make them in summer camp. Regimented leisure. In heaven I would have to beg God for a pass to visit my grandson so we could search for ant trails on maple trunks."

She regarded me sympathetically. "Randall, your fingernails would tear pearls off gates." Again the formal demeanor: "'Does heaven exist?' 'Live as if it does not.'" Without stopping to absorb this idea, I decided to try my hand at a ditty. But after seeking a rhyme for "heaven," I gave up after "leaven."

"The idea that this world is a snare or a stepping-stone, Randall—you know, a bubble or a vapor—I'd call that an abomination."

As we enjoyed a long pause, two quasi-Quakers, I burst out: "You may search all over heaven, but you'll find no 57." Her expression—puzzled? Amused? Indulgent? Instead of explaining, I changed the topic. "About this life, Unfaith—I mean, to make the most of it, how do you think we—"

"'First, do no harm.' That's a command we stole. Hurt nobody, behave morally, feel bad when we don't, and ameliorate what we can." I agreed with all those provisions, yet I felt some kind of twinge. Wasn't her response a little—removed? Was it even fully…. "But of course," I thought, "she's not human." I doubted her power over concerns that weighed upon me—suffering, stunted lives, hardship, oppression, vulnerability, endurance, unhappy endings…. At times I felt their canvas straps digging into my shoulders.

"'What is a heart?'" I found myself asking aloud. "'A rarity and a liability.'"

"Bless you, Brother Randall! I should let you know—I'm what we call a 'visitant.' I minister to those in the sticks, literal or spiritual."

A long silence, during which I fondly remembered a Bahai'i acquaintance who took the bus around Wyoming to encourage the faithful. I thanked her. She stretched her goggles downward, snapped them, wiggled them in place, and surveyed the horizon. "You're welcome. Good clouds for flying—cumulus humilis. A downdraft you don't want."

Filing this advice, I asked her to wait a second, hustled back in, and carried out a folding stool: "This will help you get onto the rail."

"To be frank, I'm better at takeoffs than landings." As she put boots to treads, I steadied her hand as a wing pushed against my upper arm with more than a little heft. "Randall," she asked, "is there something else you want to tell me?"

"Yes!"

"Please take another idea back to your assembly—"

"Featherhood."

I let it pass. Another Q & A was coming upon me. "'What is the first duty of religion?' 'To prevent violence.'" I ventured to add a corollary: "'Shall any faith countenance it or base itself thereupon?' 'No.'" Then I dared another. "'Or threaten it?' 'No.'"

She regarded me with a touch of amazement. "This concern—how long has it been working on you?"

"Ever since a morning like this some years ago when a flock of the devout took wing toward paradise and caused woe, like in the poem." The fruits of their effort, I thought with uncouth contempt, were seventy-two cherries.

She took a breath. "Let me be clear—there is no guarantee that we secular angels can do any more than Writ-flitting Figments. Randall, it seems to me that—that you have a calling."

Here comes the bell," I thought ruefully. On this adventure would I get boots that fit? "As a visitant?" I asked, and held my breath.

"No, Randall, as an *author*. I am commissioning you to write a book." I heard myself exhale.

"A book."

"Here's a good title." Up went the quotation marks: "'Scriptures Kaleidoscopic and Chthonic.'" I wanted to bite my arm. "Uh…. What does—"

"No, wait! What do you think about 'Earthly Scriptures'?"

Now the proposal sparked my curiosity. "Unfaith, I appreciate your—confidence. I am in fact honored."

She smiled, then turned to examine the sky while balancing on the rail and holding my upraised hand. I asked if she knew the way back. "Yes, I have a landmark, a 'Jesus Saves' boulder." No doubt that outcropping painted scarlet and white next to a country church.

"I guess it was in God's plan," I declared, "when he made the Appalachians." She laughed and plummeted headfirst.

"Jesus God!" She sank toward the top of the foliage—but her wings sprang open and glistened to the north and south, as just in time she pulled out of the dive with a mighty beating. When she reached the field, she veered from her straight line into a counterclockwise arc; I realized that she was circling the vehicle that, however derelict, had managed to outrun its color. Then she resumed her trajectory and became smaller and smaller, a twist of bittersweet vine trailing from her left boot, her wings undulating. I stifled a prayer for her safety.

Hearing an automobile climb the hill, I joyfully recognized my wife, raced to dispose of the telltale vessels, and from the floor snatched up the weightless, inkless shape of a quill.

CPSIA information can be obtained at www.ICGtesting.com
Printed in the USA
BVIW12n0927051117
499503BV00009B/64